Kirstenbosch Gard

GROW
NERINES

A GUIDE TO THE SPECIES, CULTIVATION
AND PROPAGATION OF THE GENUS *NERINE*

Text by Graham Duncan
Photographs by Graham Duncan except where credited

Right: *Nerine masoniorum* from the Eastern Cape is critically endangered in the wild

Below: *Nerine laticoma* in habitat, Northern Province

CONTENTS

Laurian Brown

Marieta Visagie
2000.

4

A BRIEF HISTORY

The glittering autumn blooms of *Nerine sarniensis*, widely considered the most beautiful of all the nerines, has an equally colourful history. The often-told, but unlikely tale of how boxes of bulbs of our most famous *Nerine*, consigned for Holland, washed up on the shores of Guernsey in the Channel Islands in 1659 as a result of a Dutch or English shipwreck, and flourished there, has become something of a botanical legend. Actually, the plant was originally thought to have been a native of Japan! The phrase name *Narcissus Japonicus Rutilo Flore*, which accompanied the first description and illustration of this species, published in 1635 by the Parisian physician, Jacob Cornut, was based on a plant which flowered in the garden of Jean Morin in Paris in October 1634, and clearly attests to its supposed Japanese origin. It was Robert Morison, Professor of Botany at Oxford, who can be held responsible for the mistaken origin of this species as it was he who suggested in 1680 that it had established itself on the coast of Guernsey after being cast away from a sinking ship, *en route* from Japan. The mistaken assumption that this species originated in Japan almost certainly stems from confusion with the superficial resemblance of the rose-red or scarlet flowers and similar strap-shaped foliage of the

Above: *Nerine sarniensis*, reddish-orange form in habitat, Western Cape

Left: Scarlet form of *Nerine sarniensis* from the Western Cape. Reproduced from the original watercolour by Marieta Visagie

Above right: Deep rose-pink form of *Nerine sarniensis* from the Western Cape

NERINE SARNIENSIS
BETTY'S BAY 152/75   1982

1. INFLORESCENCE 2. BULB WITH BULBLETS & IMMATURE LEAVES 3. FRUIT 4. MATURE LEAF
ALL LIFE SIZE

Morison, in an attempt to conceal any association with Lambert, may have purposely falsified the origin of the plant. In 1753, when Linnaeus published his *Species Plantarum*, he included this plant under the name *Amaryllis sarniensis*, naming it after Sarnia, the Roman name for Guernsey. Such was the conviction that Guernsey was this plant's natural home, it soon became known locally as the Guernsey lily, a name which has been steadfastly maintained until today; indeed in 1958, a 3d. postage stamp issued by Guernsey depicts our well-travelled Nerine! *N. sarniensis* has been cultivated on Guernsey for more than three centuries, and it continues to be grown there for its cut flowers. Similarly, our equally famous belladonna lily, *Amaryllis belladonna*, which has become naturalised on neighbouring Jersey, is today boldly depicted on postcards there, and resolutely referred to as the Jersey lily!

amaryllid *Lycoris radiata.* This species is endemic in Japan and is known to have occurred on surrounding hills above the port city of Nagasaki, overlooking its famous harbour.

There is an alternative, albeit far-fetched hypothesis as to the reasons for Morison's suggestion that the bulbs were of Japanese origin, as well as to how they came to be grown on Guernsey. In the 1650s, *N. sarniensis* is known to have been cultivated in the Wimbledon garden of Oliver Cromwell's Major-General, John Lambert. After the Restoration, Lambert was exiled to Guernsey, and it is likely he took the plant with him; the Royalist Robert

However, it was Francis Masson, who more than a century after its original publication, was credited with the discovery of the real native habitat of *N. sarniensis* on Table Mountain and surrounding mountains, during his expedition to the Cape in 1772. Masson had been sent to South Africa by Sir Joseph Banks, Director of Kew Gardens, as its first official plant collector, and returned to England in 1775. It was the cleric and amaryllid expert, Rev. William Herbert (1778-1847), son of Henry Herbert, Earl of Carnarvon, who first established the genus *Nerine* in 1820. It is unclear whether he named it for Nerine, the Greek mythological sea nymph and daughter of sea God Nereis and Doris, or for Nereide, the daughter of Nereus, son of Oceanus. By 1821, Herbert recognised nine *Nerine* species, and was also one of the first to work in the field of hybridising this horticulturally important genus. He recognised seven *Nerine* hybrids in 1837, all of which were first generation crosses between *N. sarniensis*, *N. undulata* and *N. humilis* (see page 49 for further historical notes on *Nerine* hybrids and cultivars). William Herbert's contribution to the knowledge of the Amaryllidaceae has been fittingly commemorated by naming the official journal of the International Bulb Society *Herbertia* after him. Two other southern African geophytes, the scarlet-flowered *Gladiolus nerineoides* from the mountains of the south-western Cape, and the heavily scented *Ammocharis nerinoides* from central and eastern Namibia, owe their specific epithets to the genus *Nerine*. In the instance of *Gladiolus nerineoides*, its flowers resemble those of the scarlet forms of *N. sarniensis*, with which it grows, and in the case of *Ammocharis nerinoides*, its flowers resemble those of the many *Nerine* species with medium-sized, pink flowers.

In 1896, J.G. Baker listed fifteen *Nerine* species in his *Flora Capensis*, and in the ensuing period up until 1966, a further twenty-one species were added, most of which were contributed by Winsome Barker, former Curator of the Compton Herbarium at Kirstenbosch, and five by Louisa Bolus, Curator of the Bolus Herbarium from 1903 to 1955. Most of these were published and beautifully illustrated in *The Flowering Plants of South Africa*. Then in 1967, Dr Hamilton P. Traub's scholarly 'Review of the genus *Nerine*' appeared in *Plant Life*, the journal of the American Plant Life Society (now the International Bulb Society), in which thirty species were recognised, placed in four

sections, with an extensive key. Mr K.H. Douglas, of Kingswood College, Grahamstown, assembled a vast store of knowledge on the genus based on extensive field research during the 1960s, 70s and 80s, and had always intended to produce a monograph, but unfortunately, this never materialised. In 1974, Mr C.A. Norris, honorary secretary of the British Nerine Society, published a very useful overview of the genus titled *The genus Nerine*, in which thirty-one species were recognised, including a simplified key, line drawings of floral types, and simplified distribution maps, bringing together the results of his literature and field researches over many years. He also maintained an excellent living collection of *Nerine* species in Worcestershire, England. Another great contribution to the knowledge of the genus has been made by Mr Cameron McMaster, Dohne Merino sheep expert and naturalist from the Stutterheim district of the Eastern Cape. His field observations of the Eastern

Kirstenbosch obtained bulbs of a dark rose-pink form of *Nerine sarniensis* with bright green leaves, thought to originate from those which reached Guernsey during the seventeenth century. The bulbs were donated by Mrs Le Pelley, whose husband owns the 165-year-old farm 'Les Vidiclins' where they grow at St. Saviour, Guernsey.

Carol Knoll

Cape nerines over many years have been of great assistance to many a botanist, and his collections form an important part of the living *Nerine* collection at Kirstenbosch.

Innumerable naturally-occurring colour forms of *N. sarniensis* exist, ranging in shades of crimson, scarlet and pink, many of which are represented in the living collection at Kirstenbosch. Also represented in the collection is the exceptionally attractive pure white form of this species, originally collected on Table Mountain in the 1920s. In 1984, a most beautifully executed painting of this plant by the celebrated contemporary botanical artist, Ellaphie Ward-Hilhorst, appeared in *Veld & Flora*, the Journal of the Botanical Society of South Africa, illustrating an article in which it was afforded the cultivar name 'Kirstenbosch White' (this painting has again been reproduced in this publication on page 6). In August 1981,

Left: *Nerine frithii* has conspicuous deep maroon appendages at the base of the stamens

Below: 'Gold dust' on perianth segments of *Nerine sarniensis* (see page 11 for explanation)

Right: *Nerine sarniensis* hybrid

GENERAL INFORMATION

Taxonomy

The genus *Nerine* is a member of the family Amaryllidaceae, closely related to another endemic, southern African genus *Brunsvigia*, and currently consists of twenty-five species, namely *Nerine angustifolia*, *N. appendiculata*, *N. bowdenii*, *N. filamentosa*, *N. filifolia*, *N. frithii*, *N. gaberonensis*, *N. gibsonii*, *N. gracilis*, *N. hesseoides*, *N. humilis*, *N. huttoniae*, *N. krigei*, *N. laticoma*, *N. marincowitzii*, *N. masoniorum*, *N. pancratioides*, *N. platypetala*, *N. pudica*, *N. pusilla*, *N. rehmannii*, *N. ridleyi*, *N. sarniensis*, *N. transvaalensis* and *N. undulata*. The genus is in urgent need of revision, as some species are very variable with intergradations between species, making identification difficult, and there is a need for a workable identification key. In this publication, the *Nerine* species have been placed into three main groups, based on the particular growth cycle they follow *under cultivation* in temperate climates. The three groups are winter-growing species, summer-growing species and evergreen species.

Growth Cycle

The winter-growing group contains four species – *N. humilis*, *N. pudica*, *N. ridleyi* and *N. sarniensis*. Their growth cycle is characterised by the emergence of flower buds in autumn, just before, or at the beginning of the winter growing period, followed by rapid vegetative growth during the winter months, and by complete dormancy during the summer. The summer-growing group consists of five species – *N. bowdenii, N. huttoniae, N. krigei, N. laticoma* and *N. marincowitzii.* Their growth cycle is characterised by the emergence of new leaves in early summer, followed by rapid vegetative growth throughout the summer, and by complete dormancy during the winter. The flowering period of these summer-growing species takes place in midsummer or autumn. The remaining fifteen species, most of which have numerous thread-like leaves and flower in late summer and autumn, are mainly summer-growing, but under cultivation remain evergreen when grown in temperate climates, or under greenhouse protection. The storage organ from which the leaves and roots grow is a tunicated bulb, with brittle, perennial fleshy roots, and is very well equipped to survive drought, as well as the natural veld fires that stimulate many species into profuse flowering.

Flowers and fruits

The inflorescence in *Nerine* is a few- to many-flowered umbel ranging in size and shape from the relatively large, almost spherical umbels of *N. huttoniae* and *N. laticoma*, to the medium-sized, laterally flattened umbels of *L. filamentosa* and *L. marincowitzii*, to the dwarf, conical umbels of *N. hesseoides* and *N. masoniorum*. The *Nerine* flower has six perianth segments, and on the basis of flower form, the genus can be divided into two main groups of species, one having flowers which are slightly irregular, and the other having flowers which are strongly irregular. The species belonging to the slightly irregular group are *N. filamentosa, N. gracilis, N. hesseoides, N. pancratioides, N. pudica* and *N. sarniensis*; the perianth segments of *N. filamentosa, N. hesseoides* and *N. sarniensis* radiate outwards in all directions and are arranged regularly, but the flower as a whole is slightly irregular due to the orientation of the stamens. The flowers of *N. pancratioides* and *N. pudica* are funnel-shaped, and *N. gracilis* has cup-shaped flowers. The perianth segments of the remaining *Nerine* species, which belong to the strongly irregular group, are arranged either with five of the segments placed above the stamens and one placed below, or with all the segments placed above and to the sides of the stamens. The position and length of the stamens in *Nerine* varies greatly among the species, from long and erect, as in *N. sarniensis*, to

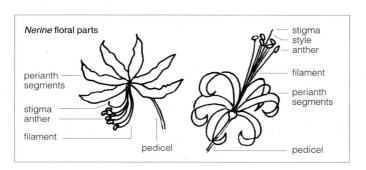

Nerine floral parts

perianth segments

stigma
anther

filament

pedicel

stigma
style
anther

filament

perianth segments

pedicel

Opposite: *Nerine humilis* dwarf form from the Western Cape (= *N. tulbaghensis*)

medium length and curved downwards or forwards, as in *N. gaberonensis*, to short and spreading, as in *N. gracilis*. Certain *Nerine* species like *N. appendiculata* and *N. hesseoides* have long or short appendages at the base of the filaments, while in others like *N. bowdenii* and *N. gaberonensis*, appendages are absent. Further, the pedicels and/or peduncle of certain species have soft short hairs, while in others this is absent. The presence and/or absence of appendages and hairs is regarded as important for the identification of *Nerine* species.

Flower colour in *Nerine* ranges through innumerable shades of pink, with darker keels, and to a much lesser extent, scarlet and white. The glittering 'gold dust' seen in bright light on the perianth segments of the scarlet forms of *N. sarniensis*, is caused by the reflection of light by the red pigment present in the epidermal cell layer, which overlays several layers of yellow pigment beneath it (Vogelpoel 1986). Similarly, the glittering 'silver dust' seen in bright light on the perianth segments of the pure white form of this species, where no pigment is present in any of the cell layers of the perianth segments, is caused by the reflection and refraction of light at the epidermal cell surfaces, and from within the cells (Vogelpoel 1997). Other scarlet-flowered monocots which also exhibit the glittering effect on their perianth segments include *Brunsvigia marginata*, *Cyrtanthus guthrieae* and *Disa uniflora*.

The development of the flower bud in the two most important commercially produced nerines, *N. bowdenii* and *N. sarniensis*, has been studied in great detail. It has been shown that at any one time, up to three inflorescence buds can be present in the bulb, each bud having been formed one year apart, therefore each bud is at a different stage of development. In both these species, the flower bud begins its development in spring, at the beginning of the summer

Left: Ripe seeds of *Nerine rehmannii* in habitat, Gauteng

Right: *Nerine filamentosa* is endangered in its Eastern Cape habitat

Right below: *Nerine krigei* has attractive, spirally twisted leaves

Carol Knoll

growth cycle in the case of *N. bowdenii*, but at the end of the winter growth cycle in the case of *N. sarniensis*. During the second growth season, the flower bud differentiates into stamens, ovary and perianth segments, and during the third growing season, the bulb flowers.

The fruit in *Nerine* is a papery capsule containing one to many round, ellipsoid, ovoid or irregularly shaped fleshy seeds, varying in diameter from 4 to 10mm. As with most other southern African amaryllids, the seeds of *Nerine* do not undergo a dormant period, and begin to germinate almost immediately after they have matured, often while still attached to the capsule wall. The water-rich seeds are able to do so by drawing on nutrients stored in the plentiful storage tissue of the seed.

Foliage

Leaf colour, shape and size varies enormously among the different species, as well as within different forms of certain species. There is variation from the bright green, arching, deeply channelled leaves of *Nerine bowdenii*, to the erect, pale green, almost flat linear leaves of *N. angustifolia*, and from the extremely narrow, dark green thread-like leaves of *N. rehmannii*, to the long, strap-shaped, spreading leaves of *N. laticoma*. Within *N. sarniensis* there is considerable variation in leaf colour and width, depending on wild locality, from dark green and relatively narrow, to broad and greyish-green, while in the very variable *N. humilis*, leaf width is very narrow in the western part of its distribution range in the south-western Cape, increasing markedly towards the eastern end of its range in the southern Cape. There are only two *Nerine* species which produce erect, spirally twisted leaves, namely the broad-leafed *N. krigei* from south-eastern Gauteng, and the thread-like leafed *N. frithii* from the eastern parts of the Northern Cape and the western and northern parts of the North West Province. The number of leaves produced per bulb often varies greatly

Cameron McMaster

within a species, as well as among different species. For example, the dwarf *N. hesseoides* may have from two to seven thread-like leaves, whereas the large *N. laticoma* may have three to twelve strap-shaped leaves. In their natural habitat, the leaves of all *Nerine* species are deciduous, and depending on the rainfall region in which they occur, are either winter- or summer-growing, with a pronounced dormant period during the corresponding summer or winter period. In cultivation, however, the *Nerine* species with numerous thread-like leaves usually remain evergreen when grown in temperate climates, or under greenhouse protection.

Distribution and habitat

The genus *Nerine* is endemic in southern Africa and its distribution extends from the north-eastern parts of Namibia southwards throughout that country to the western, southern and eastern parts of Botswana, into South Africa, where it is represented in all nine provinces. It also occurs in Lesotho and Swaziland. The Eastern Cape is home to the largest number of nerines, although not all nine species found here are restricted to this province. The very variable *N. laticoma* has undoubtedly the largest distribution of all the species, occurring over a vast area in most parts of Namibia, the western, southern and eastern parts of Botswana, as well as the eastern parts of the Northern Cape, the Free State, Lesotho, North West Province, Gauteng and the Northern Province. The species with the smallest distribution ranges are probably *N. gibsonii* and *N. masoniorum*, both restricted to very small populations in the former Transkei in the Eastern Cape, and *N. marincowitzii*, which is only known to occur in a very limited area of the Koup Karoo.

As the genus is so widely distributed in southern Africa, nerines are not surprisingly to be found in a correspondingly wide range of habitats. The four species which occur in the winter rainfall region of the Western Cape, *N. humilis*, *N. pudica*, *N. ridleyi* and *N. sarniensis*, occur in acid sandstone on sharply drained mountain slopes, which are very poor in available nutrients. Natural veld fires regularly sweep through these areas which stimulates these species into profuse autumn flowering. The aspect in which they occur is usually shady south-facing slopes, but *N. sarniensis* can also be found on the much hotter, north-west-facing slopes. The relatively large summer-rainfall species *N. huttoniae*, *N. krigei* and *N. laticoma*, as well as the smaller *N. marincowitzii*, occur in the very hot, dry inland parts of South Africa, usually in deep, fertile, alkaline sandy clays. These areas experience sudden heavy rains during summer, and subsequent vegetative growth and flowering of these nerines is very rapid, followed by heavy seed production. These species, with their relatively large, deep-seated bulbs are well adapted to withstand long periods of drought. Similarly, the small bulbs of the thread-like leafed *N. gaberonensis* are also able to survive long periods of drought, deeply wedged between the crevices of limestone and granite outcrops, or in open sand dunes in the far north-western and northern parts of the Northern Cape, southern Botswana and the western part of the Northern Province. The high altitude species *Nerine bowdenii* occurs in large colonies in loose, fibrous soil containing leaf litter, at the base of south-facing cliffs, in the high KwaZulu-Natal Drakensberg and in the midlands of the Eastern Cape. Two species with very narrow, thread-like leaves, *N. filifolia* and *N. masoniorum* from the Eastern Cape, occur in large colonies in shallow depressions in heavy clay soil on exposed rock sheets. These areas become inundated for short periods during the summer, but are very dry during the winter months.

Several species occur in black, acid soils in seasonal marshes in full sun, like *N. angustifolia* and *N. gibsonii* from the

Eastern Cape. *N. platypetala* from southern Mpumalanga, occurs at the edges of perennial marshes in heavy clay. *N. pancratioides*, from the midlands of KwaZulu-Natal, also favours moist, acid soil, and usually only flowers after veld fires.

Conservation

There are currently at least two species of *Nerine* known to be critically endangered in their natural habitats, namely *N. gibsonii* and *N. masoniorum*, both of which occur in the former Transkei in the eastern part of the Eastern Cape. The habitats of both these species have become increasingly degraded due to overgrazing and encroaching informal settlements, and it is likely they will vanish from the wild in the near future if urgent measures are not taken to preserve their habitats. Similarly, the numbers of the large-flowered *N. huttoniae*, another native of the Eastern Cape, have been much reduced due to extensive agricultural activities, but it still survives in fair numbers in isolated localities. Another rarity from the Eastern Cape is *N. filamentosa* which has a very limited distribution in the Cathcart district, where it fortunately still survives on private farmland. This species was previously thought to have become extinct in the wild until it was re-discovered by Cameron McMaster in the early 1970s. There are several *Nerine* species recorded from rather isolated parts which have been collected very infrequently, and are considered to be naturally rare, but not endangered. These include *N. marincowitzii* from the Koup Karoo in the dry Western Cape interior, *N. pusilla* from eastern Namibia, as well as *N. pudica* and *N. ridleyi* from the mountains of the south-western Cape. *Nerine platypetala* from southern Mpumalanga is another fairly rare species restricted to perennial marshes, but fortunately it enjoys some measure of protection in several wetland reserves in that area. Not so fortunate is *N. rehmannii*, whose position is becoming increasingly perilous in western Mpumalanga due to overgrazing and trampling by cattle and sheep, and in central Gauteng, where its last remaining habitat in this province is likely to succumb to housing 'development'.

The position of two dwarf *Nerine* species, namely *N. gracilis* and *N. transvaalensis*, both of which have thread-like leaves and occur in the dry inland, northern parts of South Africa, is much less certain. They have not been collected in the wild for many years, and the possibility exists that they may well be in urgent need of conservation due to agricultural expansion.

Nerine filamentosa is critically endangered in its Eastern Cape habitat

Opposite: *Nerine frithii* in habitat on a dolomitic limestone outcrop, North West Province

Left top: *Nerine humilis,* large form
from the southern Cape (= *N. peersii*)

Left below: *Nerine sarniensis*, pink
form from the Western Cape

Below: *Nerine sarniensis,* scarlet
form from the Western Cape

Right: *Nerine sarniensis*
'Kirstenbosch White' from the
Western Cape

WINTER-GROWING SPECIES

The following four species are exclusively winter-growing in their natural habitat as well as under cultivation, and undergo a long dormant period from early summer until early autumn.

Nerine humilis
(including N. breachiae, N. peersii and N. tulbaghensis)
('humilis' refers to the low-growing nature of most forms of this species)
Common names Nerine, berglelie, seeroogblom.
Distribution Clanwilliam to Worcester, Bredasdorp, Montagu to Baviaanskloof Mountains.
Height 150–350 mm.
Flowering period End of March to May.
Brief identification notes *Nerine humilis* is a very variable, widespread and gregarious species found in mountainous areas of the Western, south-western and southern Cape. The flowers are strongly irregular, and flower colour ranges from pale pink to deep rose-pink, with darker pink central keels. The perianth segments are distinctly wavy along their margins, particularly in the upper half. The bulb has a subterranean or partially exposed neck up to 40 mm long, and leaf orientation varies from prostrate to spreading or sub-erect, and leaf colour from pale to dark green or grey. In the

western part of its range, such as in the Tulbagh area of the south-western Cape, plants are dwarf, with four to five narrow, linear leaves from 60-90 mm long, and from 3-5 mm wide, and bright pink flowers borne on glabrous pedicels 10-25 mm long, on short, slender glabrous peduncles up to 120 mm long. Towards the eastern end of its range, plants become progressively larger with broader, longer leaves, up to 12 mm wide and 250 mm long, and larger, paler pink flowers borne on glabrous pedicels up to 60 mm long, and on much longer peduncles up to 320 mm high. The perianth segments of the forms in the western part of its range are much shorter and narrower, being about 22 mm long and up to 3 mm wide, whereas those from the eastern end of the range are up to 50 mm long and up to 4 mm wide. *N. humilis* grows in colonies, flowering particularly well after veld fires.

The name *Nerine flexuosa*, previously used to identify a tall-growing, winter-growing plant from the Somerset East and Grahamstown areas of the Eastern Cape, which is widely grown commercially in western Europe, has been included under the name *N. humilis*, but no alternative name has been suggested for this plant (Douglas 1985). The flowers of this Eastern Cape plant in no way resemble those of *N. humilis*, but appear to be much more closely related to another Eastern Cape species, the very variable, and complex *N. undulata*, which occurs in the same area of the Eastern Cape. Until a taxonomic revision of the genus has been completed, and the correct identity of this plant has been determined, it is suggested that *N. flexuosa* be regarded as a winter-growing form of *N. undulata*.

Cultivation *N. humilis* is an easily cutivated species, provided that it is allowed a completely dry summer dormant period, a very well drained growing medium, and a

Above: *Nerine humilis,* large form from the southern Cape (= *N. peersii*)

Opposite above: *Nerine pudica* from the Western Cape usually only flowers after veld fires

Opposite below: *Nerine humilis*

very lightly shaded or full sun position. The bulbs are planted with their necks exposed just above ground level, and like to remain in the same position for at least five years before dividing, their flowering performance improving with each successive season. The smaller forms are best suited to container cultivation, while the larger forms can also be grown in a rockery.

Nerine pudica

('pudica' refers to the concealed nature of the stamens and style)

Distribution South-western Cape on mountains from Paarl to Caledon.

Height 200-350 mm.

Flowering period March to May.

Brief identification notes The flowers of this species are unique within the genus in being more or less funnel-shaped, with the perianth segments and margins almost flat, with very little waviness. The flowers are slightly irregular, and flower colour varies from pure white to pale pink, with a darker

pink central keel visible on both surfaces, or restricted to just the lower surface. The bulb has an entirely subterranean neck up to 30 mm long and the four to six dark green, linear, sub-erect leaves grow up to 230 mm long (usually much less), and from 2-5 mm wide. They emerge soon after the flowers open. The three- to six-flowered umbel is borne atop a slender, glabrous peduncle up to 460 mm long, and has sub-erect, smooth pedicels which grow up to 38 mm long. The perianth segments vary from 25-32 mm long, and usually overlap each other by up to half their length, a character not encountered in any other *Nerine*. This poorly-known species flowers particularly well following natural veld fires.

Cultivation Although *N. pudica* is very rare in cultivation, it is grown in exactly the same manner as *N. humilis*, i.e. the necks of the bulbs should be planted just below soil level, the soil medium should be sandy and contain a little finely sifted compost,

Right: *Nerine ridleyi* is a rare, high altitude species from the Western Cape

Opposite: *Nerine sarniensis*, scarlet form from the Western Cape

and the bulbs must be allowed a completely dry dormant period from early summer to early autumn. This species is best suited to pot cultivation. The bulbs do not multiply as rapidly as those of *N. humilis*, but they flower regularly and should be left undisturbed for at least five years before dividing. A sunny position with free air circulation is required.

Nerine ridleyi

('ridleyi' commemorates Mr G.H. Ridley, a former Curator of the Cape Town Municipal Gardens)

Distribution Western Cape, from the Koue Bokkeveld to the Hex River Mountains.

Height 150-350 mm.

Flowering period February to April.

Brief identification notes The strongly irregular flowers range in shades of pink and at a glance could easily be mistaken for a pink form of *N. sarniensis*, however the stamens of *N. ridleyi* are distinctly curved downwards whereas those of *N. sarniensis* are erect, and the perianth segments of the latter are arranged regularly. The bulbs are up to one third larger than those of *N. sarniensis* and have a relatively broad, partially exposed neck up to 40 mm long. The strap-shaped leaves of *N. ridleyi* resemble those of *N. sarniensis* but are relatively short and much broader, from 80-120 mm long and 15-25 mm wide, and have blunt tips. The pedicels are smooth, 30-40 mm long, while the smooth, slender peduncle grows up to 230 mm high. The perianth segments are about

30 mm long and up to 5mm wide with deeper pink keels, and have wavy margins and distinctly recurved tips. The inflorescence bears about five to eight flowers, and plants occur in concentrated colonies at high altitude, on shady, moist, steep south-facing slopes, on acid sandstone. This is a very seldom collected and poorly known species which needs to be studied in habitat in greater detail.

Cultivation *N. ridleyi* is very rare in cultivation, and like *N. sarniensis*, its flowering behaviour is rather erratic. Its cultivation requirements are very similar to those of *N. humilis* and *N. sarniensis*, i.e. the necks of the bulbs should be placed just above soil level, the soil medium should be sandy and contain a little finely sifted compost, and they must be allowed a completely dry dormant period from early summer to early autumn. A lightly shaded position is required for this species, which

20

is best suited to cultivation as a container subject. Regular, well-spaced heavy watering is required during the winter growing period.

Nerine sarniensis
('sarniensis' refers to the island of Sarnia, the Roman name for Guernsey, one of the Channel Islands)
Common names Guernsey lily, Jersey lily, red nerine, berglelie.
Distribution North-west-and south-facing mountain slopes in the Western Cape, from Citrusdal to Caledon.
Height 250-450 mm.
Flowering period March to mid-May.
Brief identification notes The spectacular, glittering blooms of *N. sarniensis* are quite unmistakeable; the relatively broad perianth segments radiate outwards in all directions and are strongly recurved and wavy along their margins. Segment length varies up to 35 mm long, up to 6.5 mm wide, and the erect or suberect, smooth pedicels grow up to 50 mm long. The inflorescence carries from seven to fifteen flowers and the stamens stand erect and are particularly conspicuous due to the strongly recurved perianth segments. The stamens are arranged in a slightly irregular manner and there are no appendages at the base of the filaments. Flower colour ranges from crimson to scarlet and pale pink to deep rose-pink, and there is also a most attractive, pure white form known as *N. sarniensis* 'Kirtsenbosch White', which has only been recorded from Table Mountain, where it was collected in the 1920s. The glittering 'gold dust' seen in bright light on the perianth segments of the red forms of this species is caused by the reflection of light by the red pigment present in the epidermal cell layer, which overlays several layers of yellow pigment

beneath it (Vogelpoel 1986). Similarly, the glittering 'silver dust' seen in bright light on the perianth segments of the pure white form of this species, where no pigment is present in any of the cell layers of the perianth segments, is caused by the reflection and refraction of light at the epidermal cell surfaces, and from within the cells (Vogelpoel 1997). The spreading, strap-shaped leaves vary in length from 200-300 mm or more, and there is considerable variation in their width and colour, from pale to dark green or grey, and from 12-25 mm wide, depending on the form. The bulb has a partially exposed neck up to 40 mm long. *N. sarniensis* usually occurs in large colonies, always on acid sanstone. The flowers of the scarlet forms of *Nerine sarniensis* are pollinated by the mountain pride butterfly *Meneris tulbaghia*, which also pollinates the scarlet forms of other striking monocots like *Disa uniflora* and *Cyrtanthus elatus*.
Cultivation *N. sarniensis* is the most famous and the second-most widely grown *Nerine* after *N. bowdenii*, but with *N. bowdenii*, it is

also the most notorious for erratic flowering behaviour. Mature bulbs do not flower reliably every year, but it would appear that certain forms are naturally much more floriferous than others. It also seems that particular individuals from wild populations flower more reliably than others. Certainly, the effect of natural veld fires stimulates

are best planted with their necks fully exposed above soil level. It is an ideal subject for deep or shallow containers, as well as for rockeries, in sunny positions. The bulbs cannot survive long wet periods during the summer dormant period, and must be kept as dry as possible during this period.

this species to flower much more readily but the species is not dependent on fires for flowering. In order to obtain free-flowering plants under cultivation, it is necessary to constantly select and propagate only the most floriferous clones. Further, research conducted in The Netherlands has shown that light is not an important factor in determining good flowering performance, but that temperature is very important; the successful growth of the flowering stem is enhanced by relatively high temperatures at flowering time in early autumn, and optimum temperature for flowering to occur is between 17-21 °C. It is also interesting to note that new flower buds (those that will flower in future flowering seasons) are initiated in spring at the end of the growing period, and that their initiation is not dependent on temperature. This species is easily cultivated in a free-draining medium containing equal parts of river sand, loam and sifted, acid compost, and the bulbs

Left: *Nerine huttoniae* from the Eastern Cape requires a full sun position

Below: *Nerine bowdenii* from the Eastern Cape

Right: *Nerine bowdenii* from the Eastern Cape

SUMMER-GROWING SPECIES

The following five species are exclusively summer-growing in their natural habitat as well as under cultivation, and undergo a long dormant period from late autumn until early summer.

Nerine bowdenii

('bowdenii' commemorates Mr Athelstan Cornish-Bowden, who sent bulbs of this species from South Africa to England in the early 1900s)

Common names Large pink nerine, grootpienknerina.

Distribution In the high Drakensberg in western KwaZulu-Natal and in the midlands of the Eastern Cape.

Height 300-700 mm.

Flowering period January to May.

Brief identification notes *N. bowdenii* is a native of the high KwaZulu-Natal Drakensberg and the midlands of the Eastern Cape where severe winter conditions are experienced. It grows in large colonies on steep, south-facing slopes. *N. bowdenii* has one of the largest inflorescences within the genus, borne on a very sturdy, smooth peduncle up to 450 mm long. Its perianth segments are certainly the longest and widest of all the species, growing up to 76 mm long and up to 8 mm wide, and the flowers are borne on smooth, sub-erect pedicels up to 50 mm long. The perianth segments have distinctly wavy margins and darker pink keels, and the tips are distinctly recurved. The perianth segments of the *N. bowdenii* populations from the northernmost end of its range in the northern Drakensberg, known in the hoticultural trade as *N. bowdenii* 'Wellsii' are very much more wavy than those from the Eastern Cape, and these plants are generally larger and more robust in most respects. Flower colour varies from pale to deep pink, and there is also a much less common, almost pure white form from the Eastern Cape midlands, known in the trade as

Nerine bowdenii from the Eastern Cape

Opposite above: *Nerine bowdenii* in habitat, KwaZulu-Natal Drakensberg

Opposite below: *Nerine huttoniae* from the Eastern Cape flowers well in containers

N. bowdenii 'Alba'. In general appearance, *N. bowdenii* looks like a very large-flowered form of *N. humilis*, but the former is an entirely summer-growing, winter dormant species which flowers towards the end of its growing period. The bulb has a long, mainly subterranean neck up to 80 mm long and the six to eight long, strap-shaped leaves are channelled and arching, and can grow up to 300 mm long, and up to 30 mm wide. They die back in late autumn, often as the flower buds are emerging. Flower buds may however emerge at any time from mid-January until late autumn.

Cultivation *N. bowdenii* is the only truly hardy member of the genus and it is widely cultivated out in the open in the United Kingdom and in western Europe, where it withstands severe frost. It will grow where winter temperatures drop to -15 °C, provided that the bulbs are kept as dry as possible over this period. Under such adverse Northern Hemisphere conditions, the bulbs should preferably be planted at the base of a south-facing wall, in perfectly drained soil, where the eaves provide protection from rain. Additional winter protection of a dry mulch of straw, bracken litter or leaf-mould is recommended, and the bulbs are planted with their necks up to about 30 mm below soil level. In temperate parts of the Southern Hemisphere, *N. bowdenii* prefers a lightly shaded situation and not full sun, and the necks of the bulbs should rest just above the soil surface. The soil medium should comprise equal parts of finely sifted compost, river-sand and loam, and during the winter dormant period they must be kept as dry as possible. This species is also well suited to cultivation in deep containers, but over-watering soon results in the roots rotting away. The trick is to apply heavy watering at well-spaced intervals, allowing the soil

John Winter

medium to dry out almost completely in between. The medium should not remain constantly moist. However, the bulbs of this species are quite resilient and will produce new roots if treated with a fungicide and grown-on in pure river-sand for a few months. *N. bowdenii* is not a particularly reliable flowerer as mature bulbs certainly do not flower every single year. This species has been used extensively in breeding programmes and its blooms are highly recommended as cut flowers. The flowers of certain forms of this species are reported to be 'muskily' scented.

Nerine huttoniae

('huttoniae' commemorates Mrs C. Hutton who collected the type material at Sheldon on the Fish River, Eastern Cape)
Common name Hutton's nerine.

leaves which grow up to 300 mm long and up to 20 mm wide. The bulb is large, deep-seated, and has a long, entirely subterranean neck up to 70 mm long. The leaf tips of the outermost leaves wither during the summer growing period, hence their truncate appearance.

Morphologically, *N. huttoniae* differs from *N. laticoma* mainly in having small fleshy, scale-like appendages between the base of the filaments and the base of the perianth segments, and in its leaves being more concave along the upper surface. The flowers of *N. huttoniae* are strongly irregular, very short-lived, and vary in shades of light to deep rose-pink, each perianth segment with a darker pink or brown median keel. The distribution of the two species is well separated – *N. laticoma* has a very wide distribution, occurring in large colonies on flats in deep sand in central, northern and southern Namibia, southern Botswana, the Northern Province, Gauteng, the North West Province, the Northern Cape, Free State and Lesotho, whereas *N. huttoniae* is a fairly rare species restricted to the western part of the Eastern Cape, occurring in colonies near riverbanks or in seasonally damp depressions.

Cultivation Unlike *N. laticoma*, *N. huttoniae* flowers regularly in cultivation and requires a position in full sun and a deep sandy soil, to which a little finely sifted compost has been added. The bulbs should be kept completely dry during the dormant period from late autumn to late spring. It is suited to cultivation in deep plastic pots, or to pockets in a summer-rainfall rockery, and the bulbs are planted with their necks at or just below soil level. Apply heavy watering throughout the summer growing period, but allow the soil medium to dry out in between watering.

Distribution The western part of the Eastern Cape.

Height 200-350 mm.

Flowering period Late January to mid-March.

Brief identification notes This species resembles, and is closely related to *Nerine laticoma*, which has a similarly sized, many-flowered spherical umbel, and a relatively short, glabrous, compressed peduncle. It has seven to ten very similar spreading, strap-shaped, shiny dark green

Nerine krigei

('krigei' commemorates Mr J.D. Krige of Stellenbosch, who discovered this species south-east of Johannesburg in the early 1930s)

Common name Corkskrew nerine.

Distribution Occurs in south-eastern Gauteng, in damp depressions, in grassland.

Height 300-450 mm.

Flowering period January to end of February.

Brief identification notes *N. krigei* is the only species with broad, erect, spirally twisted leaves. The degree of leaf width and twisting varies considerably depending on the form being cultivated – the narrower the leaf, the greater the degree of twisting. Leaf length varies up to 270 mm long and 12 mm wide, and the bulb produces an entirely subterranean neck up to 40 mm long. The smooth, compressed peduncle grows up to 360 mm long, and produces a large, open inflorescence with smooth pedicels up to 75 mm long. Flower colour ranges from deep pink to maroon-pink, and their shape is strongly irregular. The segments are up to 37 mm long and 5 mm wide, and have wavy margins. They are recurved in the upper portion, and have darker pink keels. The long filaments are curved downwards and are deep pink or maroon-pink, and have no appendages at their bases.

Cultivation This is one of the easiest and most rewarding nerines to cultivate. It requires a full sun position, regular deep watering during the summer growing period, and will tolerate a wide variety of free-draining soils containing some well decomposed compost. The bulbs should be planted with their necks at or just below the soil surface, and should be left undisturbed for at least five years, until they become overcrowded and flowering performance diminishes. It is an exclusively summer-growing plant which undergoes a long dormant period from late autumn until early summer. Ideally, the bulbs should be kept dry during the winter dormant period, but this tough species easily withstands heavy winter rainfall, such as is experienced in the southern suburbs of the Cape Peninsula, provided that it is planted in a very well drained medium. It grows equally well in the garden or in deep containers, and is

Opposite: *Nerine krigei* does particularly well in a rock garden

Nerine krigei from south-eastern Gauteng

one of the earliest species to flower. Mature bulbs regularly produce offsets, and propagation by seed produces flowering size bulbs within three years.

Nerine laticoma

(including *N. duparquetiana*, *N. falcata* and *N. lucida*)
('laticoma' refers to the broad tuft of leaves)
Common names Gifbol, jeukui, seeroogblom.

Above: *Nerine laticoma* from the Northern Cape

Right: *Nerine laticoma* (= *N. duparquetiana*) from Namibia, does well in containers

Opposite: *Nerine marincowitzii* (from the Koup Karoo) is best grown as a container subject

Distribution The dry inland parts of Namibia, southern Botswana, the Northern Province, Gauteng, North West Province, Northern Cape, Free State and Lesotho.
Height 200–300 mm.
Flowering period Early January to late March.
Brief identification notes *N. laticoma* closely resembles another summer-rainfall species, *N. huttoniae*, which has a similar large, spherical inflorescence of strongly irregular flowers, produced on a compressed, smooth peduncle up to 400 mm long. Four to eight spreading, strap-shaped leaves are produced, which can grow up to 300 mm long and up to 15 mm wide, and grow from a large, deep-seated bulb with a long, entirely subterranean neck up to 80 mm long. The flowers of *N. laticoma* are borne on long smooth pedicels up to 100 mm long, and have white, palest pink or rose-pink perianth segments, with a conspicuous pinkish-brown median keel. The segments grow up to 45 mm long and up to 5 mm wide, and the filaments do not have the

lateral appendages at their bases which are present in *N. huttoniae*. The perianth segments of the form of *N. laticoma* previously known as *N. duparquetiana*, which occurs in Namibia and the Northern Cape, are strongly recurved in the upper part and are particularly attractive.

N. laticoma usually occurs in very large colonies in deep red sand, and has a very wide distribution stretching from central Namibia to Botswana and throughout the northern and central provinces of South Africa, whereas *N. huttoniae* is restricted to just a few localities in the western part of the Eastern Cape. The flowers of both species are rather short-lived.

Cultivation It would seem that certain forms of *N. laticoma* are not as free-flowering in cultivation as others. For example, the plant previously known as *N. duparquetiana* (now included under *N. laticoma*) flowers very well in the bulb collection at Kirstenbosch every year, yet other forms of *N. laticoma* in the collection flower much less frequently. They certainly do require

high summer temperatures and a completely dry winter dormant period to grow and flower well. Bulbs are planted with the necks at or just below soil level, and the soil medium should consist mainly of river-sand, with the addition of a little sifted compost when grown in pots. Regular heavy watering is required during the summer growth period, but it is advisable to allow the soil medium to dry out completely in between watering. *N. laticoma* is suited to cultivation in deep plastic pots, or to a summer-rainfall rockery.

Nerine marincowitzii

('marincowitzii' commemorates Mr C.P. Marincowitz of Prince Albert, who first discovered this species)

Common name Marincowitz's nerine.
Distribution In the dry Koup Karoo, Western Cape province interior.
Height 150-200 mm.
Flowering period End of March to May.
Brief identification notes This is a most attractive, rare dwarf species, which was

described as recently as 1995. The deep-seated bulb has a long, entirely subterranean neck up to 60 mm long, and produces two to six narrow, bright green, strap-shaped spreading leaves which grow up to 300 mm long, and up to 4 mm wide, and are distinctly channelled. The fairly dense inflorescence is borne on a short compressed, smooth peduncle, and produces fifteen to forty strongly irregular, very pale pink flowers with white throats, which fade to brown as they mature. The pedicels are smooth and the immature dark maroon anthers are particularly conspicuous, as is the curved, sturdy, dark maroon peduncle. The peduncle of this species is unique within the genus as it detaches at ground level when in fruit, thus allowing the wind to roll the mature inflorescence with its ripe seeds across the soil.

Cultivation In its natural habitat, *N. marincowitzii* has a rather short growing period from early to midsummer, after which it undergoes a dormant period until autumn, at which time the flowers appear. Following the flowering and fruiting period, the plants undergo a long dormant period throughout winter until early summer. Under cultivation, however, the plants can be kept growing throughout the summer until autumn, in the same way that other exclusively summer-growing species like *N. laticoma* and *N. huttoniae* are cultivated. *N. marincowitzii* is best grown as a container subject, as the bulbs would certainly rot under ordinary garden conditions. The top of the necks of the bulbs are planted just below soil level, and the ideal growing medium is two parts silica sand and two parts river-sand, and a layer of finely milled compost placed at the bottom of the container. Mature bulbs flower reliably every year. During the summer growing period, well-spaced heavy watering are required every three to four weeks, but as soon as the flower buds appear in autumn, watering must be withheld completely until summer.

Right: *Nerine angustifolia* from Mpumalanga

Below: *Nerine masoniorum* from the Eastern Cape

EVERGREEN SPECIES

Under cultivation, the following sixteen species usually remain evergreen when grown in mild climates or under greenhouse protection. However, in their natural habitats they usually undergo a long winter dormant period from late autumn until early summer.

Nerine angustifolia

(including *N. angulata*)
('angustifolia' refers to the narrow leaves)
Common names Ribbon-leafed nerine; berglelie, lematlana.
Distribution Gauteng, Mpumalanga, Swaziland, north-eastern Free State, north-western Lesotho and the Eastern Cape.
Height 300 mm-1 m.
Flowering period November to April.
Brief identification notes This variable, pink-flowered species looks very similar to *N. appendiculata* in general appearance, but the two differ in several ways; *N. angustifolia* has up to six slightly channelled, linear leaves whereas *N. appendiculata* has up to three deeply channelled, linear leaves, and further, the stamens of *N. appendiculata* have conspicuous long white appendages at their bases, which are completely absent in *N. angustifolia*. The inflorescence of *N. angustifolia* generally has far fewer flowers (less than ten) than *N. appendiculata* (up to twenty). Both

Cameron McMaster

best grown as a container subject in areas of excessive winter rainfall. The plants require well-spaced, heavy watering during the summer growth period, but much less in winter, and they remain evergreen in temperate climates.

Nerine appendiculata

(including *N. brachystemon*)
('appendiculata' refers to the long white appendages which occur near the base of the stamens)
Common names Nerine, umlukulo.
Distribution Marshy areas of the midlands and south-western KwaZulu-Natal, as well as in the Eastern Cape, usually in large colonies.
Height 600-900 mm.
Flowering period December to end of April.
Brief identification notes The flowers of the very variable *N. appendiculata* look very

species have pedicels covered with soft hairs. *N. angustifolia* is absent from KwaZulu-Natal except for the far north-western parts, and is widely distributed from Mpumalanga to the Eastern Cape. *N. appendiculata* occurs mainly in the midlands and south-western parts of KwaZulu-Natal, and in the Eastern Cape. *N. angustifolia* produces up to six erect, linear leaves which can grow to 350 mm long, and up to 5 mm wide, and the sturdy, smooth or minutely hairy peduncle can grow up to 1 m, but can sometimes be even taller. The bulb has an entirely subterranean neck up to 50 mm long. The perianth segments vary from 30-50 mm long, and up to 5 mm wide, and have distinctly wavy margins in the upper half, and recurved tips. The flowers are strongly irregular. It occurs both on flats and montane habitats in acid grassland marshes, often in large colonies.
Cultivation *N. angustifolia* grows well under cultivation but appears not to flower as readily as species like *N. filifolia* and *N. masoniorum*. It requires full sun and is

Cameron McMaster

Opposite above: *Nerine angustifolia* in habitat, Eastern Cape

Opposite below: *Nerine angustifolia* in habitat, Eastern Cape

Right: *Nerine appendiculata* in habitat, KwaZulu-Natal, usually grows in large colonies. It looks similar to *N. angustifolia* but has long white appendages at the base of its stamens

Martin von Fintel

similar to those of another very variable, pink-flowered species, *N. angustifolia* (see *N. angustifolia* above). *N. appendiculata* has deeply channelled, linear leaves, and this species can also be distinguished by the long white appendages at the base of the stamens, which are absent in *N. angustifolia*, and by its many-flowered inflorescence (ten to twenty flowers per inflorescence), as opposed to the fewer-flowered inflorescence of *N. angustifolia* (less than ten flowers). Both species have hairy pedicels. The distribution of *N. appendiculata* is centred in the midlands of KwaZulu-Natal, whereas *N. angustifolia* is absent from this province

except for the far north-western parts. *N. appendiculata* produces one to three deeply channelled, erect linear leaves up to 450 mm long and up to 5 mm wide, and a sturdy, glabrous peduncle up to 800 mm high. The bulb has an entirely subterranean neck up to 50 mm long. Pedicel length varies considerably, from 35-50 mm long. The perianth segments vary from 25-30 mm long, and from 3-5 mm wide, and the upper half of the segments is wavy and recurved. The flowers are strongly irregular.

Cultivation *N. appendiculata* requires a full sun position and well-spaced heavy watering during the summer months, but much less during winter. It remains

evergreen when grown in temperate climates or under greenhouse protection, but will go dormant if allowed to dry out completely in winter. The bulbs should be planted with the top of the neck just below soil level. It is well suited to both container and garden cultivation and likes to be left undisturbed for many years, until flowering performance diminishes.

Nerine filamentosa

('filamentosa' refers to the conspicuous long, straight filaments)

Distribution A very rare species from the eastern part of the Eastern Cape.

Height 150-300 mm.

Flowering period February to April.

Brief identification notes The perianth segments of this very distinctive, beautiful species are all rolled back for half their length, which has the effect of exposing the conspicuous, long, more or less straight filaments. The seven to twelve slightly irregular flowers are borne on spreading, long hairy pedicels up to 70 mm long, and the inflorescence shape is laterally flattened and not rounded as in *N. filifolia*. *N. filamentosa* begins its flowering period a full month before that of *N. filifolia*. Flower colour ranges in shades of pale pink, with a very deep pink zone at the base of the segments, with dark pink central keels. The peduncle grows up to 300 mm high and is distinctly hairy, and the filaments do not have appendages at their bases. The bulb has an entirely subterranean or slightly exposed neck up to 40 mm long, and produces three to four dark green, spreading thread-like leaves, which grow up to 350 mm long and up to 2 mm wide. In the early 1990s, *N. filamentosa* was included under *N. filifolia* in 'Plants of southern Africa:

names and distribution', *Memoirs of the Botanical Survey of South Africa* No. 62 (Reid and Archer 1993). The painting which illustrated the original publication of *N. filamentosa* (*The Flowering Plants of South Africa*, volume 15, plate 569, 1935) by W.F. Barker, could easily be mistaken for *N. filifolia* as it does not accurately portray the very long filaments and rolled back perianth segments, yet the accompanying description makes bold mention of these two characters. When the flowers of living specimens of *N. filifolia* and *N. filamentosa* are compared, it becomes clear that they are indeed two very distinct species. Barker's original description was based on a plant mistakenly thought to have come from Grahamstown, and subsequently also mistakenly thought to have come from King William's Town. As the plant was never tracked down in either of these areas, it was thought to have become extinct, until it was re-discovered by Mr Cameron McMaster in the early 1970s in the Cathcart district of the Eastern Cape. Plants occur singly or in small clumps in dry grassland on dolerite outcrops.

Cultivation Although this species is rare in cultivation, it has great potential as a container subject or for pockets in a rockery, or as a thick border to larger annuals or perennials. It is cultivated in exactly the same manner as *N. filifolia*. The bulbs should be planted with their necks at or just below soil level, and they multiply rapidly in a free-draining growing medium containing some finely sifted compost. They like to remain undisturbed for up to five years, until they become too overcrowded and flowering performance diminishes. Regular heavy watering is required throughout the summer growing period, but this should be decreased considerably during the winter months; in temperate climates the plants will remain evergreen during this period. Like *N. filifolia*, the bulbs can withstand heavy winter rainfall provided that the soil medium drains well.

Nerine filifolia
('filifolia' refers to the very narrow, thread-like leaves)
Common name Grass-leafed nerine.
Distribution A gregarious species occurring in many parts of the Eastern Cape.
Height 200-320mm.
Flowering period Mid-March to May (to August).
Brief identification notes *N. filifolia* is an extremely variable, floriferous species producing five to ten fleshy, spreading, thread-like leaves up to 200mm long and up to 2mm wide. The bulb produces an entirely subterranean or slightly exposed

Opposite above: *Nerine filamentosa* from the Eastern Cape flowers reliably in cultivation

Opposite below: *Nerine filamentosa* from the Eastern Cape flowers in late summer

Right: *Nerine filifolia* (white form) from cultivated origin

Right: *Nerine filifolia* flowering prolifically in a raised brick bed

Opposite: *Nerine frithii* is a rare dwarf species well suited to container cultivation

neck up to 40 mm long. The eight to fifteen strongly irregular flowers are borne on long pedicels up to 40 mm long and the sturdy peduncle grows up to 400 mm long. After flowering, the pedicels elongate, sometimes to almost double their normal length. Flower colour ranges from palest pink to deep rose-pink, and there is also a most attractive, pure white form. The perianth segments vary from 25-42 mm long, and from 3-5 mm wide, and are distinctly wavy along their margins in the upper half, and recurved. The pink forms have deeper pink keels, while the white form has pale green keels. The filaments do not have any appendages at their bases, and the pedicels and peduncle are covered with soft, short hairs. *N. filifolia* is a gregarious species, always found growing in large colonies in shallow, heavy soil which is frequently inundated, on or in between rock slabs. There is a small-flowered form of *N. filifolia* previously known as *N. filifolia* var. *parviflora*, which grows south-east of Grahamstown and has a much later flowering period, from June to August.

Cultivation This is a very common species in cultivation and not surprisingly, as it is very attractive and a completely reliable flowerer. It grows well in a wide variety of soils, and the bulbs multiply rapidly. It is ideally suited to planting in pockets in a rockery and as a thick border to larger annuals or perennials, and is also an excellent subject for shallow containers. The bulbs like a free-draining growing medium containing some finely sifted compost, and are planted with their necks at or just below soil level. They like to remain undisturbed for up to five years, until they become too crowded and flowering performance diminishes. Regular heavy watering is required throughout the summer growing period, but this should be reduced considerably over the winter period. When cultivated in temperate climates or under greenhouse protection, the plants remain evergreen throughout the winter months and are not adversely affected by heavy winter rainfall, provided that the soil medium drains freely.

Nerine frithii

('frithii' commemorates Mr Frank Frith, an English horticulturist who collected the type specimens at an unrecorded locality in 1914)

Common name Frith's nerine, vleilelie.
Distribution The eastern part of the Northern Cape and the western and northern parts of the North West Province.
Height 200-250mm.
Flowering period February to April.
Brief identification notes The flowers of N. frithii closely resemble those of another dwarf species, N. hesseoides, which also has thread-like leaves, but in N. frithii the arrangement of the perianth segments is strongly irregular, and the deep maroon appendages at the base of the filaments are shorter and joined together for most of their length. N. hesseoides has slightly irregular flowers when viewed as a whole, but the perianth segments are arranged in a regular manner and it has long, free appendages at the base of the stamens. N. frithii has white or pale pink perianth segments with deep maroon bases, with narrow or broad, brownish-maroon keels which are particularly conspicuous on the undersides of the segments. The erect or sub-erect pedicels are smooth and grow to 30mm long. The five- to fifteen-flowered inflorescence is borne on a slender, smooth peduncle up to 200mm high. The bulb has a narrow, entirely subterranean neck up to 30mm long, and usually produces two erect or sub-erect, thread-like, channelled, spirally twisted leaves, which can grow up to 150mm long, and are 1-1.5mm broad. The only other Nerine species with spirally twisted leaves is the broad-leafed N. krigei, from south-eastern Gauteng. The distribution of N. frithii and N. hesseoides overlaps in the western and northern parts of the North West Province. N. frithii occurs singly or in small groups on seasonally inundated dolomitic limestone outcrops, in full sun.

Cultivation This species is extremely rare in cultivation, and being so small, would probably only be suited to container cultivation in a free-draining, sandy medium containing a little fine, sifted compost. Being a mainly summer-growing species, heavy, well-spaced watering is required

Carol Knoll

from spring until mid-autumn, whereafter the soil medium should be allowed to dry out completely in frost susceptible areas. Like other *Nerine* species with thread-like leaves, it often remains evergreen during the winter months when grown in temperate climates or under greenhouse protection, in which case occasional watering can be applied during this period.

Katie Steel

Nerine gaberonensis

('gaberonensis' refers to Gaborone, capital of Botswana, which lies within the distribution range of this species)

Distribution In the far north-western and northern part of the Northern Cape, the southern and south-eastern part of Botswana, and the western part of the Northern Province.

Height 120-250 mm.

Flowering period Early January to mid-April.

Brief identification notes *N. gaberonensis* is one of the most attractive of the pink-flowered species with thread-like leaves, producing a small, medium or large inflorescence of five to fifteen strongly irregular flowers, borne on smooth pedicels 25-65 mm long. The peduncle is smooth and grows up to 180 mm long. The narrow perianth segments are up to 17 mm long and up to 2 mm wide, channelled, strongly recurved and wavy along their margins, and have dark pink central keels. The stamens have no basal appendages and are strongly curved downwards. The bulb has a subterranean or slightly exposed neck up to 30 mm long, and produces several spreading, thread-like leaves up to 150 mm long, and 1-2 mm wide. The leaves are usually much fleshier than those of other species with similar thread-like leaves, like *N. filifolia* and *N. filamentosa*. *N. gaberonensis* occurs in colonies, the bulbs either firmly wedged in between cracks of limestone and granite outcrops, or at the base of deep red sand dunes, in full sun.

Cultivation This rather variable, dainty or relatively robust, free-flowering species does very well under cultivation and is ideally suited to growing in pots on a sunny balcony or verandah. The bulbs multiply fairly rapidly by offsets and like to remain undisturbed for several years, until flowering performance diminishes due to overcrowding. Regular watering is required during the summer months but this should be reduced considerably during winter. When grown in temperate climates or under greenhouse protection, the plants remain evergreen. It has a very long flowering period extending from midsummer until mid-autumn, depending on the form being cultivated.

Nerine gibsonii

('gibsonii' commemorates Mr L.F. Gibson of Engcobo, who collected this species in the mid 1950s)

Common name Gibson's nerine.

Distribution A very rare species from the former Transkei, Eastern Cape.

Height 150-300 mm.

Opposite: *Nerine gaberonensis* in habitat, Northern Cape. Its stamens are distinctly curved downwards

Right: *Nerine gibsonii* is critically endangered in its Eastern Cape habitat

Flowering period April to July.

Brief identification notes The several pale green, thread-like leaves are similar to those of *N. filifolia* but are erect or sub-erect, slightly broader and channelled, and up to 20 mm long and 2 mm wide. The bulb produces an entirely subterranean neck up to 35 mm long. This distinctive species has strongly irregular flowers with relatively long, broad perianth segments up to 35 mm long and up to 7 mm wide, the perianth segments ranging in colour from pure white through several shades of pale pink to purple. The four to six pedicels grow up to 32 mm long, and the peduncle grows up to 300 mm high. Both the pedicels and peduncle are distinctly hairy, and the perianth segments each have a conspicuous dark pink central keel in the lower half. The segment margins are slightly wavy and the tips are not recurved. The filaments have distinct appendages at their bases and the deep maroon, unripe anthers are conspicuous. *N. gibsonii*

occurs along stream banks in wet, black acid soil.

Cultivation Although it grows fairly well under cultivation, this rather attractive species is not a reliable flowerer, and probably needs the effect of fire to do so regularly. At Kirstenbosch it flowers in July which is an unusual time for a *Nerine*. Its active growing season extends from early summer to mid-autumn, during which time it requires frequent watering, but much less so in winter. It remains evergreen in temperate climates if watered sparingly during the winter, but will otherwise become completely dormant. It is not as easily grown as species like *N. filifolia* and *N. masoniorum*, and certainly would not survive excessive winter rainfall. It is best grown as a container subject in a sunny position on a verandah. The leaves are particularly susceptible to attack by lily borer during the summer months, and if left unchecked, the caterpillars will proceed into the bulb which they completely hollow out.

Nerine gracilis

('gracilis' refers to the slender overall habit of this species)

Distribution Restricted to southern Mpumalanga.

Height 150-250 mm.

Flowering period February.

Brief identification notes The flowers of *N. gracilis* are easily recognised by their distinct cup-shaped appearance, with the perianth segments arranged in a slightly irregular manner. The short, broad segments are pale pink or rose-pink, each with a distinct green keel on the lower surface, and are borne on smooth pedicels 40-70 mm long. The segments have distinctly wavy margins but are not recurved. The stamens are less than half the length of the segments, and there are distinct, two-teethed appendages at the base of the filaments. The bulb produces an entirely subterranean, narrow neck up to 30 mm long, and the three to five thread-like leaves grow up to 300 mm long, and are 1.5 to 2 mm wide. In their natural habitat, the leaves grow in summer, and die back during the winter months. *N. gracilis* occurs in damp depressions in shallow soil over rock sheets, usually in large colonies.

Cultivation *N. gracilis* is seldom encountered in cultivation and really deserves to be grown much more frequently. Being a dwarf species, the bulbs are best grown as container subjects and should be massed together for best effect. The soil medium should be sandy and free-draining, with the addition of a little fine, sifted compost. Well-spaced, regular heavy watering is required during the summer growing period. Like other *Nerine* species with thread-like leaves, it remains evergreen when grown in temperate climates or under greenhouse protection, but in areas with very cold winters, it should be allowed to go completely dormant over this period.

Nerine hesseoides

('hesseoides' refers to the close resemblance this species has with the flowers of several *Hessea* species)

Distribution The western and northern parts of the North West Province.

Height 170-250 mm.

Flowering period February.

Brief identification notes *N. hesseoides* is a dwarf species, closely related to *N. frithii*, both of which have thread-like leaves and occur in the western and northern parts of the North West Province. The bulb of *N. hesseoides* has a very narrow, entirely subterranean neck up to 25 mm long, and has two to seven leaves which can grow up to 180 mm long and are 1 to 1.5 mm wide. The very slender, smooth peduncle produces a small, compact inflorescence with distinctly erect, smooth pedicels 20-30 mm long. Although the flowers are slightly irregular as a whole due to the orientation of the stamens, the perianth segments are arranged in a regular manner, as in the genus *Hessea*. The flowers rank as the smallest in the genus and are pale pink in the upper two thirds of the segments, and dark magenta in the lower third. The perianth segment margins are conspicuously wavy in the lower part, and there are long, free appendages at the base of the filaments. The closely related *N. frithii* has larger flowers, the perianth segments are arranged irregularly, and the appendages are shorter and joined together for much of their length. *N. hesseoides* occurs in colonies on limestone outcrops, in full sun.

Cultivation Like *N. frithii*, *N. hesseoides* is extremely rare in cultivation, and being

Left: *Nerine masoniorum* from the Eastern Cape

Below: *Nerine masoniorum* from the Eastern Cape is critically endangered in the wild

small, would only be suited to container cultivation in a free-draining, preferably alkaline sandy medium containing some finely sifted compost. Being a summer-growing plant, it requires heavy, well-spaced watering from spring until mid-autumn, whereafter the soil medium should be allowed to dry out completely when grown in areas with very cold winters. Like other *Nerine* species with thread-like leaves, it often remains evergreen during the winter months when grown in temperate climates, in which case occasional watering can be applied during this period.

Nerine masoniorum

('masoniorum' commemorates Marianne Mason (who collected material near Umtata in the Eastern Cape in the late 1920s) and her brother.
Common name Masons' nerine, Transkei lily.
Distribution An endangered species with a very restricted distribution in the former Transkei in the Eastern Cape.
Height 150-220 mm.

Flowering period Late January to March.
Brief identification notes This is a very distinctive, dwarf species which produces four or five spreading, thread-like leaves up to 200 mm long, and 1.5 mm wide. The bulb produces a very narrow, slightly exposed or entirely subterranean neck up to 40 mm long. The very small, compact inflorescence of pale to bright rose-pink, strongly irregular flowers is borne on a very slender, hairy peduncle. The perianth segments are very narrow and strongly

recurved, up to 13 mm long and 3 mm wide, with conspicuously wavy margins, each with a darker pink central keel. The filaments have short appendages at their bases, and the pedicels are distinctly hairy, growing up to 30 mm long. *N. masoniorum* is close to extinction in its natural habitat because of habitat degradation from encroaching informal settlements.

Cultivation *N. masoniorum* is a profuse-flowering plant, ideally suited to cultivation in pots and window-boxes, and it is also a most valuable bedding plant where it is suited to planting as a thick border to larger annuals or perennials. It is very easily cultivated and the bulbs multiply rapidly by offsets, in addition to producing copious amounts of seed. The plants prefer full sun, but will also flower well in very light shade. It is one of the earliest nerines to flower, and the bulbs like to remain undisturbed for many years, until flowering

performance diminishes. They take a year or two to establish themselves after dividing. Plants require regular watering throughout summer, but much less during winter, although they are not adversely affected by heavy winter rainfall, provided that the soil medium is well drained. They remain evergreen in temperate climates but in the wild undergo a dormant period from late autumn until early summer.

Nerine pancratioides

('pancratioides' refers to the white-flowered inflorescence which resembles that of the amaryllid *Pancratium tenuifolium*)

Common name White nerine.

Distribution In the midlands and south-western part of KwaZulu-Natal, as well as in north-eastern Lesotho.

Height 400-950 mm.

Flowering period March to April, usually only after fire.

Brief identification notes *N. pancratioides* produces a sturdy, smooth peduncle with a fairly dense inflorescence of up to twenty very distinctive, pure white, funnel-shaped, slightly irregular flowers. The pedicels are densely hairy, and grow up to 38mm long. The short stamens are less than half the length of the perianth segments, the latter being up to 24mm long and up to 5mm wide. Unlike most other *Nerine* species, the perianth segments of *N. pancratioides* are only very slightly recurved at their tips and the margins are only slightly wavy. The several linear, bright green leaves may grow up to 300mm long, 2mm wide, and are slightly channelled along most of their length, becoming flat towards the tips. The bulb produces a long, entirely subterranean neck up to 80mm long, and plants occur in moist, acid soil in rocky areas.

Cultivation *N. pancratioides* is very seldom grown, and not surprisingly, as it requires the effect of fire in order to flower. It tends to remain evergreen under cultivation in temperate climates, and does well in deep pots in an acid, sandy soil containing some finely sifted compost or milled bark. Ideally, this species should be grown in terracotta pots which can be plunged to ground level, and have some straw, grass or twigs burnt over the top once during the winter season, in order to stimulate flowering the following autumn.

Nerine platypetala

('platypetala' refers to the relatively broad perianth segments)

Common name Swamp nerine.

Distribution Southern Mpumalanga, in perennial marshes.

Height 300-400mm.

Flowering period February to March.

Brief identification notes As its specific name indicates, the perianth segments of this species are relatively broad, being up to 6mm wide and up to 26mm long. The shape and arrangement of the perianth segments is unique within the genus; the base of the segments is folded and very narrow at the base, then flares abruptly, and has a rounded tip. The segments are also distinctive in being flat, and their margins are not at all wavy. Flower colour is pale pink, bright pink at the base of the segments, with darker pink central keels. The pedicels are densely hairy, 25-60mm long, and elongate remarkably (up to 150mm in length) after the first few flowers have opened. The sturdy, smooth peduncle produces a slightly irregular inflorescence of eight to fifteen flowers. Up to nine erect or sub-erect, narrow, more or less flat, bright green leaves are produced. The bulb has

Nerine platypetala from Mpumalanga has broad, flat perianth segments

Opposite: *Nerine pancratioides* in habitat, KwaZulu-Natal, only flowers after veld fires

an entirely subterranean neck up to 40 mm long and the species occurs in very wet acidic, black fibrous soil.

Cultivation *N. platypetala* is very rare in cultivation, but it is easily grown, and is one of the most attractive summer-flowering species. It remains evergreen when grown in temperate climates, such as in the southern suburbs of the Cape Peninsula, but in the wild it undergoes a long dormant period during the cold winters. The bulbs do well planted close together in deep pots that are kept well watered throughout the summer, and mature bulbs flower reliably every year. Seed forms readily following self-pollination. Watering should be reduced considerably during winter, in which case the bulbs will remain evergreen when grown in temperate climates, but in frost-susceptible areas it is best to keep the bulbs completely dry over the winter period. *N. platypetala* can also be grown in wet areas surrounding a garden pond.

Nerine pusilla

('pusilla' refers to the small overall size of the plant)

Distribution In western and eastern Namibia, in limestone river-beds.

Height 100-200 mm.

Flowering period December, probably also at any other time during the summer depending on adequate rainfall.

Brief identification notes This is a very rarely collected species which is hardly ever seen because it only appears after erratic, good rains in its inhospitable environment. The bulb has a narrow, entirely subterranean neck up to 40 mm long, and produces two to three spreading, thread-like leaves 150-200 mm long and 0.8 to 1 mm wide. The slender peduncle produces a small, very attractive inflorescence of three to five white or pale

Carol Knoll

Nerine rehmannii in habitat in Gauteng, is a dwarf species ideally suited to container cultivation

Opposite: *Nerine rehmannii* in habitat, Gauteng, has strongly recurved perianth segments

pink, strongly irregular flowers. The perianth segments have darker brownish-green or pink central keels, and grow to 17 mm long and up to 4 mm wide. The flowers resemble those of *N. humilis*, but the pedicels of *N. pusilla* are minutely hairy and up to 25 mm long, whereas those of *N. humilis* are smooth, and the leaves of *N. humilis* are narrowly strap-shaped.

Cultivation *N. pusilla* is completely unknown in cultivation but would probably make a good pot subject, just like the dwarf amaryllid *Ammocharis nerinoides* does, which occurs in the same part of Namibia. *N. pusilla* no doubt requires a free-draining, sandy growing medium containing some finely sifted compost, and well-spaced heavy waterings during the summer growing period. Like other *Nerine* species with thread-like leaves, it would probably remain evergreen when cultivated in temperate climates, in which case occasional watering during the winter dormant period can be given, but in areas with very cold winters the soil medium should be dried out completely.

Nerine rehmannii

('rehmannii' commemorates German botanist and geographer Prof. Anton Rehmann, who discovered this species in the late 1870s)

Common name Rehmann's nerine.
Distribution On rocky outcrops in central Gauteng and western Mpumalanga.
Height 150-300 mm.
Flowering period March.
Brief identification notes This is usually a dwarf species producing two or more extremely narrow, thread-like leaves up to 90 mm long and 0.5 to 1 mm wide. The bulb produces a very narrow, slightly exposed neck up to 30 mm long. The very small, compact inflorescence of pure white flowers is occasionally flushed with pink, and the perianth segments are very narrow, up to 8 mm long and up to 1.5 mm wide, and are distinctly wavy and strongly

Carol Knoll

recurved. The segments have attractive dark maroon central keels on their undersides, which are only noticeable during the bud stage. The slender, smooth peduncle produces an umbel of up to nine, slightly irregular flowers, borne on smooth pedicels up to 8 mm long. *N. rehmannii* usually grows in large colonies and needs the effect of veld fires to clear bush and smothering grasses in order to flower well. Under ideal conditions, it propagates by producing copious amounts of seed, in addition to offsets.

Cultivation In its natural habitat, this species has a long dormant period from mid-autumn until early summer, but under cultivation it often remains completely evergreen in temperate climates. Under cultivation, bulbs multiply rapidly by offsets but it seems to be a rather shy flowerer. It is very rare in cultivation. *N. rehmannii* is best grown massed together as a pot subject on a very sunny verandah where its small, delicate flowers can be fully appreciated – it is not generally suited to garden cultivation as its flowers would be 'lost' among other garden plants, and in areas of heavy winter rainfall the bulbs would almost certainly rot. It requires regular heavy watering during summer but much less in winter.

Nerine transvaalensis

('transvaalensis' refers to the erstwhile Transvaal province, where this species is reported to occur)

Distribution In the erstwhile Transvaal, although the exact distribution is unknown.
Height up to 200 mm.
Flowering period Unknown.
Brief identification notes *N. transvaalensis* is a very poorly known species, closely related to *N. frithii*, which also has thread-like leaves. Two leaves are normally

produced, which grow up to 150 mm long and up to 1.5 mm wide, and the bulb produces an entirely subterranean neck up to 30 mm long. The smooth peduncle produces an umbel of five to seven pale pink flowers on smooth pedicels up to 30 mm long, with perianth segments spreading sideways and upwards, i.e. with strongly irregular flowers. The segments grow up to 15 mm long, and up to 4 mm wide, and the margins are slightly wavy, and form a distinct, short tube before flaring outwards. The appendages at the base of the filaments are diagnostic in being closely packed next to each other, forming a tight circle around the base of the filaments. *N. transvaalensis* is also regarded as being distinguishable from *N. frithii* on account of its slightly narrower perianth segments and longer, more slender filaments. No information is available regarding the distribution range or habitat preference of this species, having been described from a single specimen collected somewhere in the former Transvaal province, exact locality not recorded, which was figured in *The Flowering Plants of South Africa* in 1928.

Cultivation *N. transvaalensis* is completely unknown in cultivation, but it would probably be best grown in the same manner suggested for *N. frithii*, *N. gracilis* and *N. hesseoides*, as a container subject in a sandy, free-draining medium containing a little finely sifted compost, and applying regular heavy watering during the summer months, and allowing a completely dry, winter dormant period. The plants would probably remain evergreen when grown in temperate climates, or under greenhouse protection.

Nerine undulata
(including *N. alta*, *N. flexuosa*)
('undulata' refers to the distinctly wavy margins of the perianth segments)
Distribution In the western and central parts of the Eastern Cape.
Height 300-900 mm.
Flowering period April to June.
Brief identification notes
N. undulata is a very variable species as regards perianth segment length and width, degree of waviness of perianth segment margins, length of peduncle and habitat preference. The species previously known as *N. alta*, now included under *N. undulata*, which occurs in grassland in the Stutterheim, Cathcart and Kei Road areas, is easily recognised by its very long, erect peduncle (600-900 mm) and small, compact, rounded inflorescence. It has narrow, folded perianth segments 21 mm long and up to 2.5 mm wide, which are strongly undulate along their margins. Its narrow, strap-shaped leaves vary from 8-10 mm wide and from 150-200 mm long, and it grows singly in wetland marshes in full sun, as noted by Cameron McMaster. The typical form of *N. undulata*, which occurs south and east of Grahamstown, has short, narrow, folded perianth segments up to 20 mm long and 2 mm

Opposite: *Nerine undulata*
(= *N. flexuosa*, pink form) from the Eastern Cape

Left: *Nerine undulata* is more or less evergreen in temperate climates

Below: *Nerine undulata*
(= *N. flexuosa* 'Alba') from the Eastern Cape, is fairly hardy out of doors in the United Kingdom and The Netherlands

Brian Mathew

wide, which are intensely wavy along their margins. The leaves are very narrow and channelled, growing up to 260 mm long and 8 mm wide, and the long, narrow peduncle grows to 600 mm high. The plant grows in open grassland in full sun. There are several other, almost evergreen forms of *N. undulata*, which occur in the Engcobo, Adelaide and Bedford districts, which have shorter, much broader, non-folded perianth segments up to 4 mm wide and up to 18 mm long, and the inflorescence is larger, much less dense, and is borne on a shorter, stronger peduncle 300-450 mm long. Its strap-shaped leaves vary from 15-20 mm wide and from 250-380 mm long,

and it grows in clumps on steep slopes in shady forest verges, as noted by Cameron McMaster. In all forms of *N. undulata*, the flowers are irregularly shaped and the pedicels and peduncle are smooth.

The name *N. flexuousa*, previously used to identify a tall-growing, winter-growing *Nerine* which occurs from Somerset East to north-east of Grahamstown (and which is widely grown commercially in western Europe), has been included under the name *N. humilis*. However, an alternative name for this plant has not been suggested (Douglas 1985), and until a botanical revision of the genus has been completed, and the correct identity of this plant has been determined, it is suggested that this plant be regarded as a winter-growing form of the variable, complex species *N. undulata*, which appears to be its closest relative.

Cultivation The forms of *N. undulata* which grow in full sun and have short, very narrow perianth segments and narrow

in being distinctly winter-growing, and will go dormant in summer if the bulbs are allowed to dry off. However, if watering is continued throughout the year, the plants remain evergreen.

leaves, are almost evergreen, dying down for a short period in midwinter. Their bulbs like to be planted with the necks just below soil level. The forms which grow in semi-shaded locations and have broader perianth segments, are particularly free-flowering, and the bulbs multiply rapidly. They prefer a lightly-shaded position and are almost evergreen in cultivation, the leaves dying down for a short period in midwinter. Their bulbs like to be planted with the necks fully exposed above soil level. The forms of this species previously known as *N. alta* have a longer dormant period in winter, following the flowering period in late autumn and early winter. They prefer a full sun position. The plant previously known as *N. flexuosa* is unusual

Left: *Nerine undulata* (= *N. alta*) grows in wetland marshes in the Eastern Cape

Below: *Nerine sarniensis* x *Nerine humilis*

Right: *Nerine bowdenii* x *Nerine sarniensis*

NERINE HYBRIDS AND CULTIVARS

Nerine species, when grown in close proximity, hybridise very readily with one another, and consequently a large number of garden hybrids, as well as more than a thousand man-made hybrids as well as cultivars, have arisen in various parts of the world during the past three hundred years. One of the first to work in the field of *Nerine* hybridisation was Rev. William Herbert (1778-1847), son of Henry Herbert, Earl of Carnarvon, and author of the genus *Nerine* which he established in 1820. By 1837, Herbert recognised seven first generation *Nerine* hybrids, all of which were crosses between *N. sarniensis*, *N. undulata* and *N. humilis*. However, by 1896, when J.G. Baker's account of *Nerine* appeared in the *Flora Capensis*, it was reported that all the hybrids listed by Herbert had 'disappeared' from horticulture. In 1875, the English *Nerine* breeder Mansell, introduced his famous Mansellii hybrids, which were essentially crosses between *N. sarniensis* and *N. flexuosa*, which produced flowers in shades of pale purple and red. The evergreen habit of *N. flexuosa* under cultivation, resulted in all these hybrids being evergreen, some of which are still in cultivation in The Netherlands today. Baker's 1896 work listed fourteen new, named first generation hybrids which were then in cultivation, by which time several more *Nerine* species had found their way to England from South Africa, and joined the *Nerine* breeding pool. Since then, the introduction of the very hardy N. *bowdenii* to England in the early 1900s, provided *Nerine* breeders with the most valuable species of all. Today, well-known cultivars of *N. bowdenii* include the vigorous, early-flowering, pale pink 'Fenwick's Variety', the deep pink 'Pink Triumph', and two wild-selected cultivars, 'Wellsii', from the high KwaZulu-Natal Drakensberg with its dark pink, intensely wavy perianth segments, and 'Alba', the pure white form from the midlands of the Eastern Cape.

From the world-renowned gardens at Exbury in Hampshire, England, Lionel de Rothschild began an extensive *Nerine* breeding programme after World War 1, and introduced many hybrids and cultivars, principally of *N. sarniensis*. This work continued right up until the late 1960s, but subsequently it was discontinued, and the entire collection was dispersed. Sir Peter Smithers began an extensive *Nerine sarniensis* breeding programme in the 1960s and 70s in England and Switzerland, and produced numerous new cultivars, notably in the purple colour range. In 1995, his superb collection was acquired by Exbury, where the tradition of *Nerine* breeding is once again being continued by Nicholas de Rothschild. Innumerable intraspecific hybrids between different forms of *N. sarniensis* have been raised over the years, and cultivar names have been given to many wild-collected plants to distinguish the many different geographical races of this species, such as the broad-leaved, vigorous, crimson-flowered 'Fothergilli', and 'Kirstenbosch White'. The major variation of colours in *N. sarniensis* hybrids today range through

every imaginable shade of red, but there are also some excellent crosses which have produced bicoloured and multicoloured flowers.

The bright pink-flowered hybrid known as 'Hera' is a cross between those two stalwarts of *Nerine* breeding, *N. bowdenii* and *N. sarniensis*. The genus *Nerine* has been found to be compatible with the closely related genus *Amaryllis*, a result of which has been the rather gaudy, shocking pink intergeneric hybrid developed at Van Tubergen in The Netherlands, known as *x Amarine tubergenii* 'Zwanenburg Beauty', a cross between *Amaryllis belladonna* and *Nerine bowdenii*.

The major commercial *Nerine*-growing and breeding nations of today are Japan, New Zealand, the United Kingdom, The Netherlands and the USA. In The Netherlands, by far the most widely produced commercial *Nerine* is *N. bowdenii*, where the cultivars 'Favourite' and 'Van Roon' are the most important. *N. bowdenii* is by far the most important cut-flower nerine at the Dutch flower auctions, and is also currently the greatest export nerine, most of which are shipped to Japan. Currently, breeding work in The

Netherlands is centred on improving and overcoming the notoriously low flower yield of *N. bowdenii* cultivars. The glittering, strongly recurved perianth segments and prominent stamens of *N. sarniensis* have always given it very high commercial value, but because of its notoriously erratic flowering performance, and the fact that it is winter-growing and not reliably hardy in very cold parts of the Northern Hemisphere, its popularity as a commercial item ranks very far below that of *N. bowdenii*. The most important commercial cultivar of *N. sarniensis* today is the bright scarlet-flowered plant known commercially as *N. sarniensis* var. *corusca* 'Major'.

As a result of the excellent breeding work undertaken with *N. sarniensis* in several countries, the colour range in cultivars of this species today extends from deep purple through every imaginable shade of red, as well as salmon and pink, to pure white. Another species with high commercial value is the one known as *N. flexuosa* in the trade, now regarded as a form of *N. undulata*. Its reliable, free-flowering nature, long peduncles and ability to withstand some frost, as well as its tendency to remain evergreen when grown in the Northern Hemisphere, has made it a very popular subject with large scale *Nerine* growers, particularly in The Netherlands. The usual colour form of this species has rose-pink flowers, but there is also a most attractive white-flowered form known by the cultivar name 'Alba', which is reported to be hardier than the pink form and has a greater tendency to remain evergreen in cultivation in the Northern Hemisphere.

Opposite: *Nerine* hybrids

Above: *Nerine sarniensis,* scarlet form from the Western Cape

CULTIVATION

The exquisite summer and autumn blooms of nerines, combined with their general ease of cultivation and propagation has made them highly sought after throughout the world today. Many are highly prized as container and garden subjects, as well as for cut-flower production due to their suitable stem length, good flower colour and long-lasting vase life.

Aspect and climate

Most *Nerine* species require a very sunny aspect in order for successful growth and flowering to take place. Species from montane habitats like *N. bowdenii*, *N. humilis* and *N. sarniensis* prefer a situation receiving morning sun and afternoon shade, whereas grassland species like *N. filifolia* and *N. krigei*, as well as those from very dry areas like *N. huttoniae* and *N. laticoma*, thrive on full sun all day, or for as much of the day as possible. The typical form of *N. undulata* prefers a full sun aspect, whereas other forms of this species prefer light shade, and several species like *N. gaberonensis*, *N. masoniorum* and *N. platypetala* grow and flower equally well in positions in light shade or full sun. The four winter-growing species from the Western Cape, *N. humilis*, *N. pudica*, *N. ridleyi* and *N. sarniensis* do not grow well in very humid climates, whereas all the other species, including

Left: *Nerine filifolia* flowering prolifically in a raised brick bed

Opposite: *Nerine sarniensis* is an excellent container subject

those from the humid eastern parts of South Africa can be grown successfully in the dry summer heat experienced in most parts of South Africa.

Uses in the garden

Whereas all *Nerine* species can be successfully cultivated in containers, only certain species are suited to general garden cultivation, depending mainly on climatic conditions and the irrigation regime of the garden in question. In the winter rainfall region of the Western Cape, for example, tough species like *N. filifolia*, *N. krigei* and *N. masoniorum* can be grown out in the open as they easily withstand heavy rainfall during their winter dormant period, provided that the soil is well drained. However, the bulbs of species from very dry habitats like *N. huttoniae* and *N. laticoma* will soon rot under wet winter

conditions, and must be grown in pots which can be stored dry over the winter dormant period. Deciduous, winter-rainfall species like *N. sarniensis* and *N. humilis* can also be grown in the open garden, in frost-free areas, provided that the bulbs are planted where they will not receive general garden irrigation in summer, and must be kept as dry as possible over this period.

Species like *N. humilis* and *N. sarniensis* are particularly effective when planted in large groups in rockery pockets, and *N. filifolia* and the dwarf *N. masoniorum* make effective edging plants when grown as a border to larger annuals and perennials. Although molerats do not eat *Nerine* bulbs, as far as is known, it is best to plant *Nerine* bulbs in sunken wire or plastic baskets in susceptible areas, as the roots strongly resent any disturbance caused by runner-moles or molerats during the growing or dormant period. In summer rainfall areas, tough species like *N. angustifolia*, *N. bowdenii*, *N. filifolia*, *N. krigei* and *N. masoniorum* are well suited to rockery pockets, while the more delicate, dwarf species are best grown in containers. It is important to note that *Nerine* bulbs, like all other amaryllids, have perennial fleshy roots which resent disturbance, therefore once they are successfully established, bulbs should be left in the same position for four to five years, until they become too overcrowded, and flowering performance diminishes.

Container subjects

All *Nerine* species make excellent container subjects which can be grouped together on a sunny patio, or grown by flat-dwellers in sunny window boxes. In many instances, container cultivation is the only feasible manner in which to grow the more delicate, dwarf species like *N. gaberonensis* and *N. rehmannii* which are not really able to withstand the rigours of the average garden. The most striking species which are particularly recommended for container

cultivation are *N. bowdenii*, *N. filifolia*, *N. humilis*, *N. sarniensis* and *N. undulata*. With the exception of *N. huttoniae*, *N. krigei*, *N. laticoma* and *N. marincowitzii*, which usually have long necks and a fairly large bulb, *Nerine* species generally need not be grown in deep containers, as the bulbs of most species like to grow close to the surface, with the necks at, just below or just above soil level. Plastic or terracotta pots are suitable; terracotta pots are recommended for cultivation in the Northern Hemisphere and plastic pots for the Southern Hemisphere. Terracotta pots tend to dry out too quickly in the Southern Hemisphere and need much more frequent watering, so larger diameter containers are required if terracotta is the preferred material. For plastic pots, a 20 cm diam. pot is suitable for dwarf species like *N. gaberonensis*, *N. pudica* and *N. rehmannii*, while a 25 cm diam. pot is suited to larger species like *N. bowdenii*, *N. sarniensis* and *N. undulata*. A 30 cm diam. pot is suggested for large species like *N. huttoniae* and *N. laticoma*. It is important that plastic containers not be placed in areas where they will overheat on very hot days, as this can frequently result in rotting of the bulbs.

Growing medium

Excellent water holding capacity as well as perfect drainage of the growing medium are two of the most important factors when cultivating nerines, particularly in containers. Although several *Nerine* species like *N. gibsonii* and *N. platypetala* grow in poorly drained swamps and marshes which are seasonally inundated, attempting to grow these species under similar conditions simulated in cultivation is very seldom successful. Nerines are tolerant of a wide range of soil types but it is important to note that *Nerine* species should not be grown in very rich soil as under these conditions they tend to produce luxuriant foliage at the expence of flowers. Similarly, the use of liquid and granular fertilizers should not be used at all. Certain *Nerine* cultivars and hybrids are however able to tolerate rich soil. Ideally, soil pH should be slightly acid to neutral.

The most important component of the growing medium is sand, which should preferably be a medium-grained, washed river sand, available from most retail nurseries. Silica sand (swimming pool sand) can also be used in combination with river sand. For garden cultivation, easily grown species like *N. bowdenii*, *N. filifolia* and *N. krigei* will grow and flower well in most free-draining garden soils (except very rich soils) to which some organic matter like well-decomposed compost has been added. Very sandy soils like those along the Cape West Coast will need to be mulched with straw or leaf litter to conserve moisture during the summer growing period. When grown in containers, a suggested mixture for all *Nerine* species is equal parts of river sand, silica sand and finely sifted compost. Alternatively, equal parts of John Innes number 2 compost and coarse river sand is recommended. A layer of stone chips or crocks should be placed over the drainage holes at the bottom of the pot, and a layer of compost about 20 mm thick can be placed over these, into which the roots can grow, allowing the bulb to rest in the sandier mix. *Nerine* bulbs, like all other amaryllids, have perennial fleshy roots which resent disturbance, therefore once bulbs have been planted, they should be left in the same position for many years, until they become too overcrowded, and flowering performance diminishes.

Nerine filifolia (white form) from cultivated origin

Planting

The bulbs of most *Nerine* species grow very close to the soil surface, but it is important that the various species are planted at the correct depth. The winter-growing *N. sarniensis* likes its bulbs to be planted with the necks fully exposed above soil level, while those of *N. humilis*, *N. pudica* and *N. ridleyi*, like to be planted with the necks slightly above, or at soil level. The bulbs of the summer-growing *N. huttoniae*, *N. krigei*, *N. laticoma* and *N. marincowitzii* should be planted with the relatively long neck fully covered with soil, so that the top of the neck rests just below the surface. In the Northern Hemisphere, bulbs of *N. bowdenii* grown outdoors can be planted so that the tops of the necks rest up to 30 mm below soil level, but when grown in the Southern Hemisphere or under greenhouse protection, they can be planted much shallower, with the top of the neck just above soil level. All the remaining species, which have thread-like or linear leaves, and remain evergreen when cultivated in temperate climates, can be planted with the top of the necks at, just below, or just above the soil surface. The winter-growing species are planted in early autumn, before the flower buds emerge, whereas the summer-growing and evergreen species are best planted in early summer.

Watering

A sound knowledge of the three different growth cycles to which *Nerine* species belong is of the utmost importance in cultivating them successfully. The exclusively winter-growing species like *N. humilis* and *N. sarniensis* require watering from mid-autumn until early summer, followed by a completely dry, summer dormant period. For the exclusively summer-growing species like *N. huttoniae* and *N. krigei*, the reverse condition applies, with watering required from early summer until mid-autumn, followed by a completely dry, winter dormant period. Under cultivation, the *Nerine* species which produce numerous thread-like leaves and follow a summer-growing, winter-dormant growth cycle in the wild, like *N. filamentosa*, *N. masoniorum* and *N. rehmannii*, remain evergreen when grown in temperate climates. Even in the Northern Hemisphere, these species will often remain evergreen when grown in the cool greenhouse. Under these conditions they can be watered throughout the year, but the frequency of watering during the winter period should be reduced to about once per month.

When watering actively growing nerines, it is always best to water heavily at well-spaced, regular intervals, as opposed to superficial, infrequent watering. During the growing period, a heavy watering every two weeks is suggested for both winter- and summer-growing species, allowing the soil medium to dry out almost completely in between.

Feeding

Neither liquid nor granular feeding is recommended for any *Nerine* species as this has the effect of encouraging luxuriant leaf growth at the expence of flower production. The nutritional requirements of nerines under cultivation is more than adequately provided for in the compost component of the suggested soil mixture (see Growing medium on page 53).

Hardiness

The only member of the genus which is truly hardy is *Nerine bowdenii*, which comes from the high Drakensberg mountains of KwaZulu-Natal and the midlands of the Eastern Cape, where severe winters are experienced. It can tolerate winter temperatures down to as low as -15°C, provided that the soil medium is kept as dry as possible over this period. In the Northern Hemisphere, the bulbs should be planted with the top of their necks about 30 mm below soil level, ideally at the base of a south-facing wall where the eaves provide protection from rain. An additional winter protection of dry straw, bracken litter or leaf mould is recommended. *Nerine angustifolia*, and two forms of *N. undulata* (one previously known as *N. alta*, the other previously known as *N. flexuosa* 'Alba') are known to be relatively hardy in The Netherlands and the United Kingdom, but do require some protection from prolonged frost. All other *Nerine* species need the protection of the cool greenhouse when grown in countries with very cold winter conditions.

Nerine hybrids from Exbury Gardens, Hampshire

A selection of as yet unnamed *Nerine sarniensis* hybrids from the *Nerine* collection at Exbury Gardens, all bred by Sir Peter Smithers at Vico Morcote, Switzerland. Photographs by kind permission of Nicholas de Rothschild.

Laurian Brown

PROPAGATION

Propagation of nerines by seed and offsets are currently the most widely used methods used by gardeners, whereas the twin-scaling method is widely used by commercial *Nerine* producers.

Seed

Propagation of nerines by means of seed is an easy, inexpensive way of increasing stocks. All *Nerine* species produce copious amounts of seed, particularly following cross-pollination by hand. Many species, including *N. filifolia*, *N. masoniorum*, *N. platypetala*, *N. undulata* and most forms of *N. sarniensis* are strongly self-fertile and will produce ample quantities of seed without any need to hand-pollinate. However, certain species like *N. gaberonensis* and *N. pudica* require hand-pollination in order to obtain a good seed harvest. In order to hand-pollinate *Nerine* flowers, use your fingers by lightly pinching a ripe anther (the pollen must be loose and be easily removed) between the thumb and index finger until the pollen adheres, then lightly pinch the stigma of a flower on a different plant. Alternatively, dab a small paintbrush over the ripe anthers and transfer the pollen to the stigmas in the same way. Be sure to use different brushes when pollinating different species, and wash your hands if using your fingers to pollinate different species at the same time. Like most other southern African amaryllids, the seeds of *Nerine* are fleshy and develop rapidly once fertilization has taken place. Seeds take from three to four weeks to mature, and as soon as they can easily be detached from the capsules, they are ready to be harvested and should be sown immediately. Freshly harvested *Nerine* seeds can be stored in the fridge for several months, provided they are kept dry and harvested before germination has started. The seeds of *N. sarniensis* are particularly resilient and will often form tiny bulbs and leaves without being planted, if stored dry for an excessively long period at room temperature.

The seeds only start to degenerate after the first true leaves have formed.

If not harvested in time, *Nerine* seeds begin to germinate while still attached to the capsule walls, which makes handling more difficult as the brittle, developing radicle can easily be broken off.

The seeds are sown in deep seedtrays in a well drained mixture such as equal parts of river sand, silica sand (swimming pool sand) and finely sifted compost. Sprinkle the seeds evenly over the surface and cover them with a thin layer of the same mixture, and water well with a fine rose. Withhold any further watering until the

first leaves appear, then water well once every two to three weeks. The seedlings of the deciduous species should be dried off during their summer or winter dormant periods, in the same way that mature bulbs are treated. Young plants should be allowed to remain in the seedtrays for at least two years, and depending on the species, can be potted-up individually into pots at the beginning of the winter- or summer-growing period. Dwarf species like *N. masoniorum* will often flower during the second year of growth from seed, but most species can be expected to flower in the third or fourth year. Larger species like *N. huttoniae* and *N. laticoma* take at least five years to flower for the first time.

Offsets

Most *Nerine* species readily produce offsets, and this is a convenient method for the home gardener of increasing stocks which will be exactly true to type. There

are, however, several species which almost never produce offsets and have to be grown from seed, namely *N. huttoniae*, *N. laticoma*, *N. marincowitzii*, *N. platypetala* and one of the forms of *N. undulata*, previously known as *N. alta*. Conversely, many species reproduce vigorously by offsets, notably *N. filifolia*, *N. humilis*, *N. krigei*, *N. masoniorum* and *N. sarniensis*. Offsets are best separated from the mature bulbs in early autumn, in the case of the winter-growing species, like *N. sarniensis* and *N. humilis*, whereas the summer-growing and evergreen species are best separated in late spring, just before, or at the beginning of active growth. The offsets are ready to be removed if they are easily separated from the mature bulb by gentle tugging, and should not be forcibly broken away as this may damage the basal plate excessively and expose the wound to fungal infection. The separated offsets should be replanted immediately to prevent the brittle, perennial fleshy roots from drying out.

Twin-scaling

The practice known as twin-scaling is used mainly by commercial producers of nerines, in order to produce large numbers of offspring which are exactly true to type. It is usually used for the two main crops with large bulbs i.e. *N. bowdenii* and *N. sarniensis*. The procedure involves cutting a mature bulb into four or six equal parts, so that each part consists of two bulb scales attached to a portion of the basal plate. The twin scales are then treated with a fungicide like captab (e.g. Kaptan) and stored in moist vermiculite in a polythene bag for a period of twelve weeks, at 20°C. Adventitious buds will develop on the basal plate between the two scales, giving rise to new bulblets, and the scales are then planted out into compost and grown at about 17°C, in a greenhouse. The bulbs are lifted after one year and stored for about three months, whereafter they can be planted into deep trays or out into the open ground, and allowed to grow-on for a further three to four growing seasons, by the end of which flowering-size bulbs will have developed. The procedure is carried out in spring for the summer-growing *N. bowdenii* and in autumn for the winter-growing *N. sarniensis*.

Micropropagation

Propagation of nerines by tissue culture involves the use of tiny portions of the bulb scale, the peduncle as well as lateral buds. The material is placed into a special multiplication medium, with the addition of supplementary growth hormones, which promotes rapid vegetative growth. This specialised method is only used by commercial growers of nerines and is not suitable for the home gardener.

Opposite above: Twin-scaling on *Nerine sarniensis*

Opposite below: Offset (daughter) bulbs develop readily on *Nerine sarniensis*

Above: Lily borer feeding on flowers of *Nerine sarniensis*

PESTS AND DISEASES

Nerines are subject to a fairly wide range of pests and diseases, and the following measures are suggested for their control.

Pests

Lily borer (also known as amaryllis caterpillar) This is without doubt the most important pest encountered on nerines in the Southern Hemisphere. Scientifically known as *Brithys crini pancratii,* the night-flying adult female moth lays its eggs mainly on the undersides of *Nerine* leaves, as well as on flower stems and developing flower buds. The tiny caterpillars bore into the leaf, stem or flower tissue, and if left unchecked, eventually bore into and consume the bulb itself, resulting in the collapse and death of the whole plant. Large caterpillars can be picked off by hand, or affected leaves can be cut off, stamped on and placed on the compost heap. However, this method of control has limited success as inevitably some caterpillars escape one's attention. Spray with a carbaryl-based insecticide such as partially environmentally compatible Carbaryl or Karbaspray, or dust affected plants with Karbadust.

Mealybugs Nerines are very susceptible to these white, waxy sucking insects, which occur underneath the tunics of the bulb and the bulb neck, where they rapidly multiply, forming large colonies. They result in malformed flower buds and leaves, and also transmit viral diseases. They are spread from one plant to another by ants. Spraying is not particularly effective in eradicationg this pest. The best method of control is to thoroughly drench the soil with an insecticide such as chlorpyrifos (e.g. Chlorpirifos) at least twice during a growing season, in severe infestations. Mealybugs are far more prevalent in container-grown plants, particularly when grown in enclosed environments like in greenhouses, than those grown in open ground. Ants can be controlled in an environmentally friendly way by pouring neat Jeyes Fluid down the ant holes, and then washing it down with water. The process should be repeated frequently.

Slugs and snails These can do great damage to the broader-leafed *Nerine* species, and are also responsible for transmitting viral disease. Pick off the culprits by hand, or, for large plantings, keep ducks to do the job for you. (Muscovies or Dutch quackers are ideal). Alternatively, one can place broken eggshells or tobacco dust in a ring around the base of the plants. Bantam poultry such as Silkies and Pekins cause minimal

damage and are beneficial in ridding the garden of many pests like caterpillars, beetles, slugs and small snails, as well as fertilizing the soil with their droppings. Do not use chemical treatments when keeping free-range poultry.

Snout beetles These small grey beetles come out at night and feed on the leaf margins of the broader-leafed species, leaving behind bite-marks and tiny black droppings. During the day they hide in between the leaf bases and upper bulb tunics, as well as at the base of the flowers and under dry leaves on the ground. Search for the culprits during their daytime hideaways and crush them by hand, or, in severe infestations, spray with partially environmentally compatible cypermethrin (e.g. Garden Ripcord), as a full cover spray. The beetles can also be caught at night using a bright torch, but the slightest movement causes them to drop to the ground, where they become instantly camouflaged; it is best to place a cupped hand or container underneath the plant and shake the culprits off.

Thrips The summer-growing *Nerine* species with broad leaves like *N. bowdenii*, *N. laticoma* and *N. huttoniae* are sometimes attacked by thrips. These minute, narrow sucking insects are most often found on the undersides of the leaves, leaving characteristic white streaks. For severe infestations, spray with Mercaptothion (e.g. Malathion) or Tenthion (e.g. Lebaycid) as a full cover spray, ensuring that the spray mist reaches the undersides of the leaves.

Diseases

Fungal Rotting Commercially grown *Nerine* bulbs are susceptible to various fungal diseases like *Fusarium, Pythium* and *Botrytis*, which cause the roots and bulbs

to rot, and which require extensive soil disinfectant treatments. When grown in small quantities by the home gardener, these problems can generally be prevented by ensuring that the soil medium drains efficiently, and that the deciduous species are kept absolutely dry during the appropriate dormant period. A diseased bulb can usually be identified by leaves which are slow to develop, or which suddenly wilt and turn yellow. If it is suspected that a bulb is rotting, it is best to lift the bulb immediately and remove any affected parts with a clean knife, then wash the bulb thoroughly with water. If a portion of the basal plate and most of the bulb scales are still intact, the bulb can probably be saved by soaking it in a solution of Dithane M45 for twenty minutes, then allowing the bulb to dry completely,

and planting the lower half into a pot of slightly damp, pure silica sand (swimming pool sand), and placing it in a shaded, warm position. Keep the medium slightly damp and allow the bulb to remain there for several months, until healthy new roots and leaves have formed.

Viruses The *Nerine* species with strap-shaped leaves, particularly *N. bowdenii* and *N. sarniensis*, are very susceptible to viral diseases which are evident by stunted growth, as well as pale yellow, and/or pale or dark green blotches and streaking across the leaf blade. Viral symptoms are also evident in the flowers, which develop blotches of a paler colour than the normal flower colour. However, a diseased bulb will not necessarily develop both leaf and flower symptoms on the same plant. Badly affected plants should be instantly destroyed to prevent infection of healthy plants, but if this drastic measure is impossible, infected plants must be kept well isolated and regularly treated preventatively against aphids, mealybug, snails and slugs, which are the main vectors that spread viruses in nerines. Seeds harvested from infected nerines do not, as far as is known, transmit viruses, and once fresh seedling stocks are growing strongly, the infected bulbs can be destroyed. Bear in mind that viral diseases can also be unwittingly spread by humans on gardening equipment like secateurs, by transferring infected sap from infected to healthy plants, such as when cutting flowering stems.

Above: Lily borer feeding on leaves of *Nerine masoniorum*

Opposite: Snout beetle damage on leaves of *Nerine bowdenii*

Left: *Nerine bowdenii* from the Eastern Cape

Below: *Nerine bowdenii* in habitat, KwaZulu-Natal Drakensberg

Opposite: *Nerine gaberonensis* from the Northern Cape is an excellent pot subject

FURTHER READING

Archer, R.H., C.L. Craib & Gillian Condy, 1997. *Nerine platypetala. Flowering Plants of Africa* 55: 36-39.

Barker, W.F. 1932. *Nerine krigei. South African Gardening and Country Life* 22: 137.

Barker, W.F. 1933. *Nerine falcata. The Flowering Plants of South Africa* 13: t.511.

Barker, W.F. 1935a. *Nerine flexuosa. The Flowering Plants of South Africa* 15: t.561.

Barker, W.F. 1935b. *Nerine peersii. The Flowering Plants of South Africa* 15: t.562.

Barker, W.F. 1935c. *Nerine alta. The Flowering Plants of South Africa* 15: t.563.

Barker, W.F. 1935d. *Nerine humilis. The Flowering Plants of South Africa* 15: t.564.

Barker, W.F. 1935e. *Nerine tulbaghensis. The Flowering Plants of South Africa* 15: t.565.

Barker, W.F. 1935f. *Nerine breachiae. The Flowering Plants of South Africa* 15: t.566.

Barker, W.F. 1935g. *Nerine krigei. The Flowering Plants of South Africa* 15: t.567.

Barker, W.F. 1935h. *Nerine filifolia* var. *parviflora. The Flowering Plants of South Africa* 15:t.568.

Barker, W.F. 1935i. *Nerine filamentosa. The Flowering Plants of South Africa* 15: t.569.

Barker, W.F. 1935j. *Nerine masoniorum. The Flowering Plants of South Africa* 15: t.570.

Bolus, L. 1938. *Nerine frithii. The Flowering Plants of South Africa* 18: t.691.

Bolus, L. 1938. *Nerine hesseoides. The Flowering Plants of South Africa* 18: t.683.

Bolus, L. 1924. *Nerine transvaalensis. The Flowering Plants of South Africa* 4: t.132.

Bolus, L. 1921. *Novitates Africanae: Nerine frithii. Annals of the Bolus Herbarium* 3: 79.

Brown, N.R., Crowden, R.K. and A. Koutoulis, 1998. Use of tissue culture techniques for hybridisation of *Nerine. Journal of the Australian Institute of Biology* 11: 47-50.

Brown, N.R., Crowden, R.K., Gorst, J.R. and A. Koutoulis, 1999. Reproductive biology of *Nerine* (Amaryllidaceae) Part 1: *Herbertia* 54: 139-152.

John Winter

68

Brown, N.R., Crowden, R.K., Gorst, J.R. and A. Koutoulis, 1999. Reproductive biology of *Nerine* (Amaryllidaceae) Part 2: *Herbertia* 54: 153-170.

Coombs, S.V. 1948. South African Amaryllids as house plants. *Herbertia* 15: 101-112, 163.

Craib, C.L. 1996. *Nerine platypetala*: habitat studies and cultivation. *Herbertia* 51: 68-73.

Craib, C.L. 1997. Populations of *Nerine laticoma* in the North West and Northern Provinces. *I.B.S.A. Bulletin* 46: 19-21.

Craib, C.L. 1998. *Nerine rehmannii* in Gauteng and Mpumalanga. *I.B.S.A. Bulletin* 47: 6-7.

Craib, C.L. 2001. *Nerine frithii*, a graceful species from the North West Province. *Veld & Flora* 87(3):124-125.

Curtis, W. 1795. *Amaryllis sarniensis. Curtis's Botanical Magazine* t. 294.

Dahlgren, R., Clifford, H.T., and P.F. Yeo, 1985. *The Families of the Monocotyledons*. Springer-Verlag, Berlin.

Dinter, M.K. 1914. *Nerine pusilla. Neue Pfl. Deutsch-Sudwest-Afrika*, p.48.

Dold, T. & D. Weeks, 2000. *Nerine huttoniae* – a rare Eastern Cape endemic from the Fish River. *Veld & Flora* 86 (1): 14-15.

Dold, T., Cloete, E. & D.Weeks, 2000. The *Nerine* from Misty Mount – the conservation status of *Nerine masoniorum* in the Eastern Cape. *Veld & Flora* 86(4): 168-169.

Douglas, K.H. 1968. A new species of Nerine from the Transkei. *Journal of South African Botany* 34: 5-7.

Douglas, K. H. 1985. Notes on African Plants: The identity of *Nerine flexuosa. Bothalia* 15: 545-546.

Duncan, G.D. 1984. *Nerine sarniensis* 'Kirstenbosch White' – the white sport. *Veld & Flora* 70(4): 55-56.

Duncan, G.D. 1989. *Nerine*. In: Du Plessis, N.M. & G.D. Duncan, *Bulbous Plants of Southern Africa*. Tafelberg, Cape Town.

Duncan, G.D. 1996. *Growing South African Bulbous Plants*. National Botanical Institute, Cape Town.

Duncan, G.D. 2000. *Grow Bulbs*. Kirstenbosch Gardening Series. National Botanical Institute, Cape Town.

Dyer, R.A. 1937. *Nerine gracilis. The Flowering Plants of South Africa* 17: t.679.

Dyer, R.A, 1942. *Nerine bowdenii. The Flowering Plants of South Africa* 22: t.841.

Dyer, R.A. 1950. *Nerine duparquetiana. The Flowering Plants of Africa* 28 t.1118.

Dyer, R.A. 1952. *Nerine huttoniae. The Flowering Plants of Africa* 29 t.1130.

Griffiths, M.(ed.). *Nerine*. In: *The New Royal Horticultural Society Dictionary of Gardening*, pp. 313-314. Macmillan, London.

Herbert, W. 1820. *Nerine rosea. Curtis's Botanical Magazine* 47: t.2124.

Herbert, W. 1823. *Nerine pulchella. Curtis's Botanical Magazine* 50: t.2407.

Hooker, W.J. 1871. *Nerine pudica. Curtis's Botanical Magazine* 27: t.5901.

Killick, D.J.B. 1990. *A Field Guide to the Flora of the Natal Drakensberg*. Jonathan Ball and Ad. Donker Publishers, Johannesburg.

Lighton, C. 1973. *Cape Floral Kingdom*, p.26. Juta & Company Limited, Cape Town.

Merxmueller, H. 1969. *Nerine Herb. Flora of South West Africa*, 150: 11. Verlag J. Cramer, Germany.

McNeil, P.G. 1971. An undescribed *Nerine* from the S.E. Transvaal. *South African Journal of Botany* 37: 267-268.

McMaster, J.C. 1976. *Nerine filamentosa*. *Veld & Flora* 62: 20.

Norris, C.A. 1974. *The genus Nerine*. *Bulletin of The Nerine Society* 6: 7-31.

Norris, C.A. 1980. *Virus in nerines. Bulletin of The Nerine Society* 6: 5-6.

Norris, C.A. 1980. *The search for Nerine*. *Veld & Flora* 66(2): 51-53.

Phillips, E.P. 1913. *Contributions to the flora of South Africa. Nerine ridleyi. Annals of the South African Museum* 9: 126-127.

Pole Evans, I.B.(ed.)1923. *Nerine rehmannii. Flowering Plants of South Africa* 3: t.120.

Pole Evans, I.B.(ed.)1924. *Nerine lucida. Flowering Plants of South Africa* 4: t.134.

Pole Evans, I.B.(ed.)1924. *Nerine flexuosa. Flowering Plants of South Africa* 4: t.139.

Pole Evans, I.B.(ed.)1929. *Nerine sarniensis. Flowering Plants of South Africa* 9: t.355.

Pole Evans, I.B. 1937. *Nerine angustifolia. Flowering Plants of South Africa* 17: t.658.

Pooley, E. 1998. *A field guide to Widflowers: KwaZulu-Natal and the Eastern Region*, pp.106-107 & 346-347. Natal Flora Publications Trust, Durban.

Reid, C. and R.H. Archer, 1993. *Nerine* Herb. In: T.H. Arnold & B.C. De Wet (editors), Plants of southern Africa: Names and Distribution. *Memoirs of the Botanical Survey of South Africa* No. 62.

Retief, E. & P.P.J. Herman, 1997. Plants of the northern provinces of South Africa: keys and diagnostic characters. *Nerine*, pp. 41-42. *Strelitzia* 6, National Botanical Institute, Pretoria.

Sealy, J.R. 1955. *Nerine angustifolia. Curtis's Botanical Magazine* (new series) 170: t.244.

Shillo, R., A.Ronen, Z. Muchnik and M. Zaccai, 1997. Improving flowering rates in *Nerine bowdenii* by moderating summer temperatures. Proceedings of the Seventh International Symposium on Flower Bulbs. *Acta Horticulturae* 430: 155-160.

Smith, C.A. 1966. *Nerine* Herb. *Common names of South African plants*. Dept. Agricultural Technical Services, Pretoria.

Smithers, P. 1999. A Brief Note on the History of Breeding in *Nerine sarniensis*. *Bulbs* 1(1): 7-8.

Snijman, D.A. 1995. A New *Nerine* Species (Amaryllidaceae tribe Amaryllideae) from the Koup Karoo, South Africa. *Novon* 5: 103-105.

Snijman, D.A. 2000. *Nerine*. In: P. Goldblatt & J. Manning, Cape Plants – a conspectus of the Cape Flora of South Africa. *Strelitzia* 9, National Botanical Institute, Cape Town.

Snijman, D.A. 2000. *Nerine*. In: O.A. Leistner (ed.), Seed plants of southern Africa: families and genera. *Strelitzia* 10, National Botanical Institute, Pretoria.

Systema, W. 1971. Effect of storage and date of planting on flowering and bulb growth of *Nerine bowdenii*. *Acta Horticulturae* 23: 99-105.

Systema, W. 1975. Flowering and bulb growth of *Nerine bowdenii*. *Acta Horticulturae* 47: 241-249.

Theron, K.L. and G. Jacobs 1994. Periodicity of inflorescence initiation and development in *Nerine bowdenii* W.Watson (Amaryllidaceae). *Journal of American Society of Horticultural Science* 119: 1121-1126.

Traub, H.P. 1967. Review of the *genus Nerine* Herb. *Plant Life* 23: 3-32.

Van Brenk, G. and M. Benschop, 1993. *Nerine*. In: De Hertogh, A. and M. Le Nard (eds), *The Physiology of Flower Bulbs*. Elsevier, Amsterdam.

Van Druten, D. 1956. *Nerine appendiculata. The Flowering Plants of Africa* 31(2) t.1211.

Vogelpoel, L. 1986. Flower Colour – an appreciation. *South African Orchid Journal* 17(3): 109-114.

Vogelpoel, L. 1995. Some observations on Pigments of Plastid Origin. *South African Orchid Journal* 26(2): 55-59.

Ward, B. 2001. Virus in Nerines, Part 1. *Journal & Proceedings of The Nerine & Amaryllid Society* (April-June edition): 6-9.

Martin von Fintel

Above: *Nerine krigei*

Right above: *Nerine appendiculata* in habitat, KwaZulu-Natal, looks similar to *N. angustifolia* but has long white appendages at the base of its stamens

USEFUL ADDRESSES

Botanical Society of South Africa

By joining the Botanical Society of South Africa, one can take advantage of its annual catalogue of surplus seed supplied by the National Botanical Institute. Seeds of *Nerine* are not generally included on this list due to their limited storage life, but at the Botanical Society's annual Garden Fair held in March, one can usually purchase bulbs of several *Nerine* species. The Society's quarterly journal *Veld & Flora* lists several specialist bulb nurseries in its classified advertisements, some of which offer *Nerine* species from time to time, and carries regular articles on bulbous plants. Further information can be obtained from:

Botanical Society of South Africa
Private Bag X10, Claremont 7735
South Africa
Tel: +27 (0)21 797 2090
Fax: +27 (0)21 797 2376
E-mail: botsocsa@gem.co.za
Website: http://www.botsocsa.org.za

Indigenous Bulb Association of South Africa

Membership of the Indigenous Bulb Association of South Africa (IBSA) will keep you in touch with others interested in bulbs. The Association publishes an annual *Bulletin* and holds meetings, outings and talks. IBSA distributes a large variety of seed of bulbous plants and bulbs/corms, including nerines, from time to time, but

only to members. Membership is open to any and every bulb enthusiast. Its aim is conservation through cultivation, and members grow a wide range of rare species.
Further information on IBSA can be obtained from:
The Secretary
IBSA
P.O. Box 12265
N1 City 7463
South Africa
Tel/Fax: +27 (0)21 558 1690

International Bulb Society, Inc.
Membership of the International Bulb Society (IBS) will allow you to participate in the IBS seed and bulb exchange. The International Bulb Society, Inc., is a non-profit organization. Said corporation is organized exclusively for educational and scientific purposes, and especially to promote, encourage and foster the horticulture, development and improvement of bulbous or geophytic plants and public interest theirin. The Society publishes an annual journal, *Herbertia*, the most comprehensive journal on bulbous plants in the world, as well as a quarterly magazine titled Bulbs.
Membership of the Society will allow you to participate in the seed exchange program, as well as the e-mail Bulb Forum.

Further information on IBS can be obtained from:
IBS Membership Director
550 IH-10 South, Suite 201
Beaumont, Texas, 77707
United States of America
E-mail: membership@bulbsociety.org
Website: http://www.bulbsociety.org

The Nerine & Amaryllid Society
The aims and objectives of the Society are the promotion of the growing and study of the whole range of the family Amaryllidaceae, with the species and cultivars of the genus *Nerine* in particular. The Society's journal *Amaryllids* is published several times per year.

Further information on The Nerine & Amaryllid Society can be obtained from:
The Secretary/Editor
The Nerine & Amaryllid Society
2 The Grove, Ickenham, Uxbridge
Middlesex UB10 8QH
United Kingdom
Tel: +44 (0)1895 464694
Fax: +44 (0)1895 235365
E-mail: ukhortic@ukhorticulture.org

Nerine bowdenii x *Nerine humilis*

Opposite above: *Nerine angustifolia* from Mpumalanga

SOURCES OF SUPPLY

South Africa

Cape Flora Nursery
P.O. Box 10556
6015 Linton Grange
Tel: +27 (0)41 379 2096
Fax: +27 (0)41 379 3188
E-mail: capeflora@iafrica.com
Website:
www.users.iafrica.com/c/ca/capeflor

The Croft Wild Bulb Nursery
P.O. Box 1053
4930 Stutterheim
Tel/Fax: +27 (0)43 683 2796
E-mail: croft@eci.co.za
Website: www.eci.co.za/stutt/croft/

Karoo Desert National Botanic Garden
P.O. Box 152
6850 Worcester
Tel: +27 23 347 0785
Fax: +27 23 342 8719
E-mail: karroid@intekom.co.za
Website: www.nbi.ac.za

Kirstenbosch Garden Centre
P O Box 53445
7745 Kenilworth
Tel: +27 (0)21 762 1621
Fax: +27 (0)21 762 0923
E-mail: kbranch@botanicalsociety.org.za

Penrock Seeds and Plants
P.O. Box 70587
2021 Bryanston
Fax: +27 (0)11 462 1998
E-mail: mwpenroc@mweb.co.za
Website: www.gisa.co.za/penroc/index.htm

Showers of Flowers (formerly Sunburst
Flower Bulbs)
P.O. Box 218
7690 Franschhoek
Tel: +27 (0)21 534 0435
Fax: +27 (0)21 534 0436
E-mail: showers-of-flowers@webmail.co.za

Simply Indigenous
P.O. Box 292
0232 Skeerpoort
Tel/Fax: +27 (0)12 207 1077
E-mail: indigenous@icon.co.za
Website:
www.simplyindigenous.garden.co.za

United Kingdom

Newchurch Nerines
Springbank Nurseries
Newchurch, Sandown
Isle of White
P036 OJX
Tel: +(01983) 86 5444
Fax: +(01983) 86 8670

GLOSSARY OF TERMS

amaryllid: member of the family Amaryllidaceae

anther: the tip of a stamen which produces pollen

appendage: a small, usually narrow attachment or projection

declinate: curved downwards or forwards

ellipsoid: solid, with sides curved equally from the middle

endosperm: storage tissue in the seed

exserted: protruding conspicuously

filament: the stalk of a stamen

gregarious: growing together in colonies

inflorescence: the flower cluster

infructescence: the mature inflorescence containing ripe seeds

keel: a longitudinal ridge

linear: long and narrow

monocot: plants producing a single seedling leaf

ovoid: egg-shaped

pedicel: the stalk of a flower

peduncle: the stalk of the inflorescence

perianth: the two floral whorls considered together

prostrate: growing closely along the ground

pubescent: downy, with short soft hairs

recurved: bent backwards

stamen: the filament and anther together

sub-: prefix denoting almost

umbel: an inflorescence with pedicels radiating outwards from a central point

Above: *Nerine laticoma* (= *N. duparquetiana*) from Namibia

Left: *Nerine gaberonensis* in habitat, Northern Cape, grows in deep red sand dunes or in cracks of limestone and granite outcrops

Opposite: *Nerine angustifolia* flowering *en masse*, Eastern Cape

Adam Harrower

INDEX

Cameron McMaster

Left: *Nerine filifolia* (pale pink form) on rock sheets, Eastern Cape

Opposite above and below: *Nerine bowdenii* in habitat, KwaZulu-Natal Drakensberg

Cameron McMaster